After the Water Dries:
A Little Book on Continual Christian Living

After the Water Dries:
A Little Book on Continual Christian Living

Joshua Seth Houston

Heart and Soul Publications
2020

First Printing: 2020

ISBN 9781706759058

Heart and Soul Publications
Murfreesboro, TN 37129

Dedication

To all who have come to faith in Christ and thought, "Now what?"

To my father John Houston and my mother Lynda Gayle Houston. Thank you for always being godly examples and guiding me along my path when I did not know what to do.

To H. A. Beasley (the man who baptized me), Ronald Harper (my first full-time ministry co-worker), and John Miller (a minister who took a special interest in my goals). Thank you for your continual help along my spiritual journey.

Joshua Seth Houston

Table of Contents

Before You Get Wet

"He saved us, not because of works done by us in righteousness, but according to his own mercy, by the washing of regeneration and renewal of the Holy Spirit"
Titus 3:5

"And there is salvation in no one else, for there is no other name under heaven given among men by which we must be saved."
Acts 4:12

"Salvation belongs to the LORD."
Psalm 3:8

Each one of us has a decision to make. We all have to face this choice at one point or another. We must ask, "Will we or will we not become a Christian?" For most people the answer has already been given. You see, if you are not living according to the word and will of God in every aspect of your life to the best of your human ability, you have already decided not to be a Christian. Sadly, most people do not understand the option to be a Christian exists in the first place.

While it is true that this book is written to be somewhat of a crash course guide for those who have already been baptized into Christ, it is important for us to first understand *why* we decided to get baptized in the first place. In other words, we need to understand what is so great about salvation.

The Problem of a Good God

The famous preacher Paul Washer is well-known for saying, "The only problem man has is that God is good." But why would this be a problem? Wouldn't we want a good God? Essentially, if God is not completely good then he is really not God at all. We need a good God to make a good creation (Gen 1:31). We want God to be good so that his intentions for us will also be good. However, the problem does not intrinsically rest with God being good. The problem is that God is good and we are not.

Romans 3:23 is almost as famous of a passage as John 3:16. Paul writes here, "for all have sinned and fallen short of the glory of God." Paul further says in Rom 6:23, "the wages of sin is death." Therefore, if all have sinned (which Paul clearly says all people have and will), then all deserve death because no one is good except God alone (Rom 3:10). This presents a major problem to the human condition. There is a deep, vast barrier between the human and God. Paul puts it in this way. He writes, "And you were **dead** in your trespasses and sins" (emphasis added; Eph 2:1). In other words, our heart may be beating, our lungs may be taking in oxygen, our mind may be functioning, but our *soul* is dead. Understanding the severity of this state is usually what brings people to ask, "How can I become right with God? Is it even possible?" Let's ponder the latter question for a moment.

Fortunately, it is possible to become right with God. Paul has an interesting way of putting it when he says that God is both just and the justifier of the one who has faith in him (Rom 3:26). This seems at first glance to be a contradictory statement. The Greek philosopher, Aristotle, defined *justice* as giving to someone that which is due them. Therefore, it would be a just thing to sentence a murderer to life in prison. However, it would also be a just thing to pay money to the one who mows your lawn. Thus, if I deserve death because of my sins (Rom 6:23), death is the only *just* thing for God to give. But to be *justified* is vastly different. Justification means that God not only makes the sinner right with him, but he also *treats* the sinner as if he is right with him. This may sound a little complicated, so let me explain.

Let's say you have taken out a loan of $10,000 to buy a vehicle. The bank has given you two years to repay the loan. If you do not pay the loan off in the allotted amount of time, the bank will seize your car. Those are the terms—plain and simple. You understood those terms and signed your name on the dotted line at the bottom of the page. However, as time passes, you realize it is almost impossible for you to pay this debt. You sheepishly walk into the bank ready to hand over the title to your beloved vehicle to the bank's possession. However, the president of the bank approaches you and offers to fully pay off your debt. You graciously thank the man and leave with a debt totally paid, not to mention you get to keep your car.

This is usually where the illustration of God's grace and mercy ends; however, there is something this illustration is missing. It is true that God has "paid our debt" with the blood of Jesus (1 Pet 1:18–19). However, if you went back to the same bank and asked for a second loan, the bank would likely not give you the loan because of your poor history. They would refuse your request because of what the president of the bank had previously done for you. God is not like this. God has not only paid our debt, but he now treats us as if we are right with him. God holds no grudges or records of former wrongs once we find ourselves in Christ.

So, God is just and the justifier of those who have faith in him. Though we may understand now that this fact is a possibility, we must ask a more difficult question. *How* is this possible? How can God exert his justice and make one right with him without giving out the full extent of what is due?

God can do this because he took the punishment of death himself. John 3:16 perfectly shows exactly what God did. "For God so loved the world that he gave his unique son that whosoever believes in him should not perish but have life eternal" (author's own translation). Did you notice the two verbs illustrating what God did? God *loved* and God *gave*. Who did God love? He loved the world. Did you know that means you? God loved you so much that he *gave*! What did he give? He gave himself. Only God himself could satisfy the wrath that is due to us. Jesus Christ (i.e., God incarnate; John 1:14) took the whole wrath of God as a perfect sacrifice and died for our sins.

Remember when Jesus was praying in the garden before his crucifixion? Remember what Jesus asked of God? He said this: "My Father, if it be possible, let this cup pass from me; nevertheless, not as I will, but as you will" (Matt 26:39). When we read this, we often neglect to remember what was actually in the cup. Some would say the pain of crucifixion was in the cup. Others would say the shame of being spat upon and mocked was in the cup. Neither of these are correct. Many Christians would later be crucified for their faith. Even Christians today are mocked and prodded for their faith. No, it wasn't any of that. It is exactly what should have been poured out on us. The wrath of God was in the cup. Jesus, being God himself, knew exactly what that wrath would entail. It would mean death and separation from the Father. However, Jesus, in his humility and obedience, went to that cross. He didn't go just to die a cruel and torturous death, though the death he faced was cruel and torturous. He went to receive the full wrath of God for you and for me.

We Are Sinners

The word "sin" means very little to most people today. The word has lost its danger. If one saw a sign that said "DO NOT CROSS! DANGEROUS BRIDGE" one would likely turn around and walk the other way. There is a clear and present danger that lies up ahead. However, Christians and non-Christians alike have a desire to run toward sin. Our human nature desires evil. That's exactly what sin is. Sin is evil.

If I were to approach you on the street and say, "I love you my friend. You mean a lot to me. It is because of this love that I want you to know the truth about yourself. You, my dear friend, are a sinner," chances are these words would go in one ear and out the other. The magnitude of the statement would not be felt or remotely understood. But imagine if one word was changed in that dialogue.

"I love you my friend. You mean a lot to me. It is because of this love that I want you to know the truth about yourself. You, my dear friend, are evil." That will make your heart sink, won't it? Evil? You mean like the Joker or Lex Luthor? No. Evil like Satan. Evil like humanity. Evil like that which is wholly opposed to God. It is because of this evil that humanity needs a savior. We have already seen how God, in his justice, should sentence us to death. However, there is one thing that is yet to be explored. It is the one thing that comes between us and our sin: Jesus Christ.

Jesus Christ and His Blood

So far, we have established two very fundamental truths. First, God is good, just, and righteous. Second, we as human beings are evil (Rom 3:23). This poses an equation of sorts.

God's goodness + my evil = man's biggest problem.

If you haven't figured it out by now, man's biggest problem is separation from God caused by sin. Man needs a savior. That's what led you to the waters of baptism in the first place. That's why you chose to have your sins washed away. Further, we noticed that only God himself can solve this problem. God did so through his son, Jesus. His death, burial, and resurrection provide salvation for all who are obedient to his command and his will.

Imagine you have gone out to dinner with some friends. You're dressed nice with a white oxford shirt and a brand-new tie (perhaps a new dress for the lady readers). You're enjoying the conversation as you begin your meal, only to realize that you have dropped tomato sauce onto your shirt. There is no way to hide the stain. It is there for everyone to see. The only way that stain will ever be completely removed is if it is washed with the appropriate materials—water and detergent. If you took your shirt or dress home and threw it in the washing machine but put in no detergent, the stain would not come out. Along those same lines, if you threw the shirt and detergent in the machine but did not add water, the detergent would do nothing. It is imperative that you have both the water and the cleansing agent to completely remove the stain.

Our souls are stained with sin. The only way according to the Bible to become clean is through water and a cleaning agent—water and the blood of Jesus. Both of these things ran out from the side of Jesus at his crucifixion (John 19:34). It is to his side that we must go. We must come in contact with his blood by means of the water. Understanding then that Jesus's blood is the only thing that can make us clean, how then does one become washed in the blood of Jesus?

What is Baptism and Why Does It Matter?

I assume (since you have this book) that you have put on Christ in baptism. However, I do not want to assume too much. It may be that you have never heard about baptism before this moment. Perhaps you have heard about it, but you do not fully understand what it is or the Bible's teaching on it. Let's break this down. Hopefully by the end of this chapter, you will firmly know what you need to do to be right with God. At the least, you will have a firm confidence in what you have done already.

Baptism, at its root, means to wash by immersion in water. Basically, the word has the idea of a dirty dish being plunged into a bucket of water, being scrubbed, then being pulled out clean. That is exactly what happens to our soul when we are baptized. Before baptism, the soul is stained with sin. Baptism is the means by which sin is removed from the soul (Acts 22:16), but more on that later.

I want to begin by exploring what may be perhaps the most famous passage on baptism in the Bible. Most likely, you heard this verse quoted when you were thinking about becoming a Christian. You guessed it…Acts 2:38, "Repent and be baptized every one of you in the name of Jesus Christ for the forgiveness of your sins and you shall receive the gift of the Holy Spirit." This verse may not seem like it means all too much at the start. It likely just seems like some guy telling some other guys what to do. As we evaluate this text, we want be sure our evaluation is based on the text's proper context. To do this, we must trace the text back to the beginning of the book of Acts.

Before Jesus ascends back to the Father, he tells the apostles what their role will be in the world. Acts 1:8 gives both the outline for the book of Acts and the outline of the spread of the gospel. "You will be my witnesses in Jerusalem, Judea and Samaria, and to the remotest parts of the world." Therefore, the gospel message begins in Jerusalem.

Acts 2 opens with the day of Pentecost. Pentecost is a Jewish holiday that celebrates the harvest of the first fruits. It is held fifty days after the Passover celebration. Therefore, fifty days have passed since Jesus's death, because, as you recall, Jesus died on Passover. What has been happening during this time? Within approximately two months, Jesus has been making appearances as a resurrected man. He appeared to the women at the tomb (Mark 16:1–8), to the apostles while they were in hiding (John 20:19–23), to Thomas (John 20:24–29), to the two men on the road to Emmaus (Luke 24:13–35), and to 500 others at one time (1 Cor 15:3–7). Jesus was ensuring that there would be no way for anyone to doubt the truth of his resurrection. Sadly, people still doubt anyways.

Fifty days have passed since Jesus's death. When Acts 2 begins, we find the Holy Spirit coming upon the apostles allowing them to speak in languages they have never studied or known. The apostles now understand that Jesus, God, and the Spirit are on their side. The apostles are on fire for the gospel (Acts 2:2–4). It is in this mighty spirit that the apostles break their silence, come out of their hiding, and proclaim the good news that can only be found in Jesus Christ.

While each of the apostles proclaimed the gospel message on that day, we only have the words of Peter recorded in Acts 2. However, we can infer that the apostles as a unified group would have also been preaching some variation of the same message. Peter's message (Acts 2:14–36) is short, simple, and to the point. While it may take modern readers a little bit of time and study to understand the message, Peter's original Jewish audience would have understood his words perfectly.

Peter's message was simply this: "You killed the son of God, the kingdom-bringer, the promised messiah." Further, Peter elaborates on the prophecies well-known to his audience and explains how Jesus is the fulfillment of these prophecies. At the end of his sermon, Peter says, "Let all the house of Israel therefore know for certain that God has made him both Lord and Christ, this Jesus whom you crucified." Many interpreters take this verse to mean that because the Jews had killed the son of God (i.e., God himself), they are now in direct opposition to God. In other words, they have sinned so badly by crucifying Jesus that there is no way for them to be made right with God, thus prompting the question of v. 37, "Men and brethren, what shall we do?" However, this I think misses the Jewish nature of the problem. Yes, the Jews certainly had committed murder, but they have done something even more problematic. You see, the messiah (i.e., the anointed one; the Christ) was to be the one who would establish the kingdom of God. The Jews were looking for a mighty warrior to defeat the Roman world power and establish the kingdom of David on Earth. Since the Jews had killed the kingdom bringer, their problem is this: "What are we going to do about the Kingdom of God?"

This is really the nuance of the question in v. 37. After hearing Peter's sermon, the people around him asked each other, "What are we going to do?" In this situation, I'd say that's a pretty good question to ask. It is the same question many (if not all) of us asked before we came to a saving relationship through obedience to the gospel. If we are lost in our sin and trespasses like Eph 2:1 says, how can we be made right with God? Peter gives the answer in v. 38.

Peter said to them, "Repent and be baptized every one of you in the name of Jesus Christ for the forgiveness of your sins and you shall receive the gift of the Holy Spirit." These same commands and promises are extended to us today. These are the necessary things one must do in order to be made right with God. Let's break this verse down a little further.

Repent

The first word in the verse is "repent." In Greek and in English, the word is an imperative verb. This means the verb is a command. In its original language, *repent* simply means to "change the mind." If you found yourself in a burning building, you would only flee the danger if your mind had been changed about your surroundings. Every action comes as a result of the mind. This is why Paul tells us to set our minds on things above (Col 3:2). In order to properly *repent*, we must change our minds concerning three different perspectives: (1) how we view God, (2) how we view sin, and (3) how we view ourselves.

I will not elaborate further on how we must view God. This was established earlier when we discussed the problem of a "good God." If you need to go back and review that section, please do. It is vital to understanding the term *repent*. We cannot view God as the bearded grandfather in the clouds. He is not that (note Paul's sermon in Acts 17 to the Epicurean and Stoic philosophers). He is love, grace, mercy, justice, and wrath all wrapped up into one benevolent being. Of course, this does not fully expound on who God is, but in short, we must know that God is good.

Therefore, we must change our minds about sin. For most of us, if we were truly honest with ourselves, we don't have a hatred of sin. Instead, we have a hatred of the consequences of sin. In other words, sin is fine to us as long as there are no negative repercussions. We can tell the little white lies because no one will get hurt. We can take a few dollars from someone. They won't miss it. Do you see the severe problem with this mindset? It assumes *some* sin is okay. Let me say this very emphatically, SIN IS NEVER OKAY. Sin is what separates us from God. Psalm 5:5 says that God hates all those who do evil. Think about that. It is not only that God hates sin. God hates **sinners**. Understanding this reality means that we must hate sin as well, not just the consequences of sin.

Lastly, we must change our minds about ourselves. The modern world has placed a significant amount of emphasis on the self. We are accustomed to exalting ourselves to places of prominence. This, in itself, is not necessarily a bad thing. As Paul says, "A laborer is worthy of his wages" (1 Tim 5:18). However, the point here is that a repented mind must understand that the human soul is tainted with sin. Our minds must be fixed on things above. The mind must be the starting point of daily living in Christ. That is really the basis of this book. Learning how to live every day for Christ begins with learning how to condition your mind.

Be Baptized

The next verb in Acts 2:38 is the passive imperative verb "be baptized." This verb is also a command. It must be noted that a **command** is not something that can be ignored. There are many religious people today who suggest baptism is not necessary for salvation. However, it is clearly commanded here. Further, Matt 28:19 gives Jesus's command to make disciples. Two participles (i.e., verbal adjectives) describe how disciples are made. Jesus says disciples are made by "going" (participle #1) and "baptizing" (participle #2). Therefore, according to Jesus, baptism must be part of how one becomes one of his disciples.

Baptism serves many purposes in its one single action. It serves as the means by which sins are removed from the soul (Acts 22:16). It serves as the means by which one enters the body of Christ (1 Cor 12:13). It signifies the death, burial, and resurrection of Jesus (Rom 6). It signifies the circumcision of the heart (Col 2:12). Each of these must be explored further, even if only briefly.

When Paul recounts his own Jesus encounter in Acts 22, he mentions the words of a man named Ananias who came to him and told him about salvation. (For more on Ananias, see Acts 9:10–19). Ananias's words in Acts 22:16 still ring true today, "Why do you wait? Get up and be baptized washing away your sins calling on his name." Baptism serves two purposes here. The first is to wash our sins away. Remember, sin is a stain on the soul. A stain can only be removed by water and a cleaning agent. Both blood and water ran out of the side of Jesus (John 19:34). Both blood and water are needed to wash away sin. Baptism then is the means by which the blood of Jesus is met.

Baptism also adds the believer to the body of Christ. Look at what Luke records in Acts 2:41, "So those who received his word were baptized, and there were added that day about three thousand souls." Being added to the church means being added to the body of Christ. There is no insignificant or unnecessary member of his body.

Think back to when Saul was persecuting the church. When Jesus appeared to Saul in Acts 9:4, Jesus said, "Saul, Saul! Why are you persecuting me?" Saul did not nail Jesus to the cross. He did not spit on Jesus. He did not beat Jesus. But he was persecuting his church—his body. These words of Jesus should encourage us. When we hurt, Jesus knows and hurts with us.

Imagine you have woken up in the middle of the night. You stumble out of bed and make your way to the kitchen for a glass of water. Along the way, you stub your littlest pinky toe on the end of the bed. Your heart begins to race, your breathing becomes labored, you reach down to grab your toe all while hopping up and down on your other foot. Only your littlest toe is hurt but your whole body knows it and reacts to it.

Some of us are the littlest toe in the body of Christ. That does not mean we are insignificant. On the contrary, we are called to do the things no one ever thinks about. We are vital for the body to be properly balanced. Paul makes this clear in 1 Corinthians 12. We do not all have the same gifts but all our gifts are needed for the growth and prosperity of the body of Christ.

When I use the phrase "obey the gospel," I imagine some of you may not know exactly what I mean, and I don't blame you. The first time I really thought about this phrase caused me to become genuinely confused. I was always taught that the gospel was the good news of Jesus, that the gospel is Jesus's ability to take away sin, and that the gospel is the death, burial, and resurrection of Jesus. It is easy to obey a command, but how then does one obey an action? How does one obey the gospel?

Paul explains this in Romans 6:1–4. I strongly encourage you (if you haven't already) to read all of Romans 6. This will give you a much better idea of the limited discussion we can have here. Paul begins Romans 6:1 by asking a simple question. "Are we to continue in sin so that grace may abound?" In other words, shouldn't I keep sinning so the grace of God will continue to cover my sins? Paul answers this question with an emphatic "OF COURSE NOT!" Those who have been baptized are dead to sin and alive in Christ. We die with him. We are buried with him. We are raised to walk, not as we once did but to a new life of repentance. Baptism serves as the means by which we put to death the old self and put on the body of Christ (Gal 3:27).

Lastly, we need to discuss this whole deal about the circumcision of the heart (Col 2:12). For modern readers of the Bible, that may be a weird thing to think about. We know circumcision was the marker of the males of God's people in the Old Testament (cf. Gen 17:10–14), but that was a literal surgical procedure. What does circumcision of the *heart* mean for Christians?

Circumcision is the removal of fleshly things that serve no purpose and can cause disease and infection. It is the removal of that which is useless. In the same way, circumcising the heart serves as the removal of useless things. Literally, it is cutting away those things that cause us spiritual harm. This is accomplished through baptism. By being baptized, we have made the decision to cut away the evil and worldly things from our lives.

Every One of You

One of the most beautiful things about this verse is that every single person is included in the command. When Peter added the caveat, "every one of you," he did not intend that command to apply only to the Jews who heard his words. Throughout the book of Acts, gentiles are also given the ability to become Christians. Think about it. You and I are likely gentiles. Most of us, I would assume, do not trace our lineage back to Abraham. The same was true for a man named Cornelius—a man who was taught the gospel by Peter (the same guy whose words are found in Acts 2:38).

Acts 10 gives us the Cornelius narrative. He was an official in the Roman army and is called a devout man. Actually, Cornelius is called a "God fearer"—a gentile who worshiped the God of the Jews without obeying the food laws or becoming circumcised. Cornelius was an important person in his culture. He was a morally good guy who believed in the one true God. However, he wasn't saved. To make matters more complicated, he was a gentile. Thankfully, God sends Peter to Cornelius to teach Cornelius the gospel. This seems simple enough. There's only one problem. Peter displays the same attitude as the prophet Jonah—he didn't really want to go. You see, Peter was a great Jew. He had been a devout Jew his whole life. He knew that the promise of God to Abraham, Isaac, and Jacob was the promise for the Jews. Unfortunately, Peter failed to realize that all are one in Christ.

So, with some persuasion, Peter eventually goes to the house of Cornelius. There, he teaches Cornelius and his family the gospel of Jesus. Things seem to be going exactly as we might expect; yet, something different happens. The Holy Spirit falls on Cornelius and his family *before* they are baptized. But don't worry. There isn't a contradiction in Scripture here. God allows this to happen for one reason and one reason only. God allows this to happen so Peter will have his eyes opened to the reality that the saving grace of God is now available to all who believe. Notice what Peter said in Acts 10:34, "Truly I understand that God shows no partiality." It is for this reason that Peter's own words "every one of you" in Acts 2:38 apply to us just as strongly today.

In the Name of Jesus Christ

There are many people today who try to say that we can be saved by many other things besides Jesus Christ. Our world says we can find peace and happiness in things like money, drugs, alcohol, and sex when the reality is that none of those things provide true peace for the weary soul. It is only in Jesus that true peace is found. Peter thus commands that baptism be done in the name of Jesus. But why?

It's really simple. The reason we must be baptized in the name of Jesus is simply because there is no other name by which we can be saved. Mohammed cannot save you. Buddha cannot save you. The president or the government cannot save you. Your job cannot save you. Money, sex, and drugs cannot save you. Only the blood of Jesus is powerful enough to make you right with God.

For the Forgiveness of Your Sins

This clause answers the question of why one must be baptized in the first place. We are baptized "for the forgiveness of sins." While there are those who say that we are to be baptized because our sins have already been forgiven, the syntax of the Greek in this text (i.e., the way words work in a sentence) disagrees with this theory. Syntactically, the word "for" is functioning in a state of advantage meaning the result (or the last part of the phrase) will be "for the advantage" of the subject. Here, the subject is the general audience of Peter's words (i.e., every one of you). Therefore, baptism and repentance are linked together by this preposition of advantage.

Now, we must establish what this advantage is. We repent and are baptized in the name of Jesus Christ *for the advantage of* having our sins forgiven. Again, this seems self-explanatory from the nature of the verse itself. However, it is so vital to understand what exactly is happening before you can move on to live a life that is totally for the Lord.

Forgiveness is more than simply saying, "I forgive you." While words are important, the forgiveness that God gives is unlike any forgiveness we can know. The Bible makes it abundantly clear that only God can forgive sins. Jesus faced this criticism in Mark 2:5–7 when Jesus forgave the sins of the paralytic. The Scribes who refuted Jesus knew that only God could forgive sins. Therefore, Jesus (a human being) is clearly claiming to be God—blasphemy! We know that Jesus is both fully human and fully God; however, that was only just being revealed to them at that time. I bring this instance to our attention not only to focus on Jesus as being truly God, but to illustrate that forgiveness echoes the true character of God.

Only God can take away sin. He is able to do this because of what he did at the cross. According to the law of Moses, God could only accept a sacrifice if it was the firstborn male from the flock/herd without blemish. While this is true for the sacrifices of the OT, Jesus was the perfect sacrifice because, though his body was beaten and marred (not physically unblemished), he was without sin. He is the only sacrifice that can actually take away sin. Hebrews 10:4 and 10 expound further on this point.

> V. 4 "For it is impossible for the blood of bulls and goats to take   away sins"

> V. 10 "And by that will we have been sanctified through the offering of the body of Jesus Christ once for all."

And You Will Receive the Gift of the Holy Spirit

The final clause of the verse gives the result that comes from both repentance and baptism. There is a lot of confusion concerning the Holy Spirit and his role within the life of the Christian. While it is not the scope of this book to discuss the work of the Holy Spirit, it is vital to know three things about his purpose in the life of the Christian.

First, the Holy Spirit serves as a pledge for the promise of God that is to come (cf. Eph 1:13–14). That may not mean much to you because the word "pledge" seems like a rigid, technical term. Think about it this way. Imagine you are going to purchase a brand-new car from a local dealership. The car costs $50,000 but you only have $10,000. The dealership will allow you to put the $10,000 as a down payment which serves as a promise that the rest will be paid when it comes due. That "down payment" is the same thing as a "pledge." In other words, the Holy Spirit serves as God's "down payment" to his people. The Holy Spirit is the promise that sins are forgiven and that Heaven is waiting.

Second, the Holy Spirit dwells within the Christian. 1 Corinthians 3:16 and 6:16 both say that our bodies are temples of the Holy Spirit who dwells in us. The Old Testament makes it clear that the temple (or tabernacle) had to be pure, holy, and ceremonially clean. In the same way, we are to be pure, holy, and righteous. That's really what this book is all about.

Lastly, we become partakers of the fruit of the Spirit. Notice what Paul writes in Gal 5:19–24.

Now the works of the flesh are evident: sexual immorality, impurity, sensuality, idolatry, sorcery, enmity, strife, jealousy, fits of anger, rivalries, dissensions, divisions, envy, drunkenness, orgies, and things like these. I warn you, as I warned you before, that those who do such things will not inherit the kingdom of God. *But the fruit of the Spirit* is **love**, **joy**, **peace**, **patience**, **kindness**, **goodness**, **faithfulness**, **gentleness**, **self-control**; against such things there is no law. And those who belong to Christ Jesus have crucified the flesh with its passions and desires.

We either walk according to the flesh or according to the spirit. If we have been baptized into Christ, the fruit of the Spirit should be evident in our lives. Paul makes it clear that there is no law against any of these things. They are and always will be morally acceptable. When we have the Holy Spirit, we have peace, joy, love, self-control, etc.

Saved by Grace?

There is a popular teaching that comes as a result of Paul's words in Ephesians 2:8, "For we are saved by grace through faith and not of our own works lest any man should boast." Doesn't this mean that I don't have to be baptized to be saved? Paul didn't say we are saved by baptism. He said we are saved by grace. Is this a biblical contradiction? Does baptism mean something else?

I bring up this issue simply because it has caused a lot of confusion and false teaching concerning salvation. Before we get into the meat of how we can walk daily with God, we need to first be confident in our own salvation. It is true that Paul said we are saved by grace. But what exactly does that mean? In order to answer this question, we will need to explore what grace is, why it matters, and how we receive that grace.

What is grace? Many would say that grace is the act of receiving something good though it is not deserved. While that is true, I think grace goes much deeper. Here is my own working definition. Grace is a gift that is not deserved, but that gift must be both freely given and freely received. The last two parts of this definition are the most vital. The gift must be freely given. If it is forcibly given, it cannot be grace. Grace comes only as the result of love. On the other hand, grace must be freely received. If it is not freely received but is received out of obligation or forced to be received, it cannot be considered grace. Therefore, grace rests on the willingness and the love of the giver to give and the willingness of the receiver to receive.

So, what is the grace of God? Perhaps we should instead ask: What is the gift of God that is not deserved but is freely given and must be freely received? The answer is simple. It is Jesus Christ.

Remember John 3:16? "For God so *loved* the world that he *gave* his one-of-a-kind son that *whosoever* believes in him should not perish but have life eternal." This verse provides all the elements of grace and attributes the gift to Jesus. The gift of Jesus is an act of love to *whosoever will*. Therefore, Jesus has been freely given and must be freely received.

So, we have established in a few short paragraphs that grace is in fact what saves us because we cannot save ourselves. But how do I come in contact with the grace of God? Do I just keep living the way I am living? Do I pray a prayer? Do I ask Jesus to come into my heart? No. As a matter of fact, no place in the Bible mentions asking Jesus to come into your heart or praying a prayer to receive Jesus. You see the point is not for Jesus to come into our heart but for us to be in the body of Christ (Gal 3:27). So, how do we freely receive the grace of God?

There are two passages that I think will help us fully understand how the grace of God is received. The first is 1 Peter 3:21–22. After explaining how Noah and his family were saved through the water, Peter says this: "Baptism, which corresponds to this, now saves you, not as a removal of dirt from the body but as an appeal to God for a good conscience, through the resurrection of Jesus Christ, who has gone into heaven and is at the right hand of God, with angels, authorities, and powers having been subjected to him." In the same way that God saved Noah *through* the water (because the flood saved Noah and his family from the evil that was on the Earth), so too baptism saves us from evil. Notice Peter doesn't say that a prayer saves us. Why? Because baptism is the means by which we are saved. Baptism is the way in which we come in contact with the grace of God. Baptism is not a physical bath that makes the flesh clean. It is an appeal to God for a good conscience because the blood of Jesus has now washed our sins away.

The last passage I wish to discuss is found in Acts 22. We have already referred to this passage many times, but it is significant to see the example yet again. Paul is recounting how he came to be a Christian. In his story, he mentions a man named Ananias who was sent to Paul for one specific purpose—to tell Paul what he must do for the Lord (cf. Acts 9:10–16). When Ananias came to Paul, he laid his hands upon Paul and said, "Brother Saul, the Lord Jesus who appeared to you on the road by which you came has sent me so that you may regain your sight and be filled with the Holy Spirit" (Acts 9:17). When Paul tells his own story, he mentions that Ananias told him, "And now why do you wait? Rise and be baptized and wash away your sins, calling on his name" (Acts 22:16). We know Paul was obedient to this based on Luke's words in Acts 9:18. "And immediately something like scales fell from his eyes, and he regained his sight. Then he rose and was baptized."

Notice what Paul doesn't do. He doesn't pray a prayer asking Jesus into his heart. Instead, he is baptized calling on the name of Jesus. Paul fully fulfills the initial command of Peter in Acts 2:38. In addition, Paul teaches the same process whenever he preaches in the book of Acts. Here are some examples for you to look at on your own. When you read these verses, be sure to also look at the whole context of the narrative.

1. Acts 16:15 → Paul preaches to Lydia and she was baptized.
2. Acts 16:33 → Paul preaches to the Philippian Jailer and he is baptized.
3. Acts 18:8 → Paul preaches to Crispus and the Corinthians who believed and were baptized.
4. Acts 19:3 → Paul preaches baptism in the name of Jesus (not John) to the Ephesians and they are baptized.

Baptism as an Outward Sign of Inward Faith?

There is another popular teaching in today's "salvation theory circle" that says baptism is just an outward sign of inward faith. In other words, baptism is just the proof that one has faith in Christ Jesus. However, there are many issues with this view of baptism. I wish to expound on some of them here.

The Bible never attributes baptism as equivalent with proving one's faith. In fact, faith is a requirement to become a part of the family of God in the first place (Rom 10:14). We need to take a step back and think really hard when we hear phrases or doctrines that are not found explicitly in the Bible. So, if baptism is not the way I prove my faith, how then can I prove my faith?

1 John 3:9 says that the one born of God (cf. John 3:1–15) no longer sins. That doesn't make any sense though because we know that everyone, even Christians, sin. John even makes the explicit statement in the first and second chapters of 1 John that Christians still sin. This is why we must confess our sins to one another. Fortunately, Jesus blood cleanses us from all sin as long as we are walking in the light (1 John 1:7), but more on that in later chapters. Jesus's blood can do this because he is our advocate with God (1 John 2:1–2). The point John is making here is not that Christians will never sin, but that one born of God should look like his heavenly father. John says in 1 John 3 that we are either children of God or children of the devil. The point is that we will look like our spiritual father, whomever that might be. Therefore, the Christian lives a life that avoids sin as much as possible because God is our father.

Paul writes in Ephesians 2:10, "For we are his workmanship, created in Christ Jesus for good works which God prepared before time, in order that we might walk in them." Paul adds in Gal 6:15, "For neither circumcision counts for anything, nor uncircumcision, but a new creation." In other words, in Christ we are new creation. The old has died. The new is here to stay. According to Paul, this new creation is created in Christ for the purpose of doing good works. We give our hearts to God for him to shape and mold into what he wants us to be. He ultimately wants us to be doers of good works on his behalf.

Lastly, James writes, "faith without works is dead" (Jas 2:26). In the course of James's letter, he eloquently explains that one cannot say they have faith but do nothing to show it. Baptism, therefore, cannot be a way to prove faith. Instead, proving our faith involves daily living for Jesus Christ.

Conclusion

Before we can even discuss our actions "after the water dries," it is vital that we understand what got us in the water in the first place. Our sin, the righteousness of God, the love of Jesus, and the grace of God that ties it all together unite in the watery rebirth that is baptism. As this chapter comes to an end, let me reiterate three things we discussed and end with three additional questions.

1. Baptism is clearly commanded in Scripture (Acts 2:38; Matt 28:19–20; 1 Pet 3:21; Acts 22:16).
2. Baptism and grace must be viewed as connected rather than two separate entities.
3. Baptism is the *only* way our sins can be removed from the soul.

The purpose of this book is to aid in your daily walk with the Lord as a new Christian. As we will see in later chapters, the walk is not an easy one. It may be that, as you are reading this section, you have never been baptized for the forgiveness of your sins. You may have been baptized as a baby (this doctrine is not found in Scripture) or as a ritual to join your local congregation (this doctrine is also not found in Scripture), but have you been baptized for the reasons that are presented in Scripture in the way Scripture demands (i.e., immersion into water)? I want to ask you three simple questions. Please answer honestly.

1. Can you be cleansed if you are not washed?
2. Can you be saved if you are outside the body of Christ?
3. Are you ready for your sins to be washed away and to become a part of the body of Christ?

If you are ready to be baptized, please don't wait. Call a minister or an elder in the Lord's church to study more or assist you further.

If you've already done this, hopefully now you have a firmer grasp on why you were baptized and what being baptized is all about.

Personal Reflection

1. Why were you baptized?
2. What do you think of when you consider a good God?
3. How do you think you can best be used in the Lord's church?
4. What is your understanding of your current relationship with God?

Zombie Faith

"What shall we say then? Are we to continue in sin that grace may abound? By no means! How can we who died to sin still live in it? Do you not know that all of us who have been baptized into Christ Jesus were baptized into his death? We were buried therefore with him by baptism into death, in order that, just as Christ was raised from the dead by the glory of the Father, we too might walk in newness of life. For if we have been united with him in a death like his, we shall certainly be united with him in a resurrection like his. We know that our old self was crucified with him in order that the body of sin might be brought to nothing, so that we would no longer be enslaved to sin. For one who has died has been set free from sin. Now if we have died with Christ, we believe that we will also live with him. We know that Christ, being raised from the dead, will never die again; death no longer has dominion over him. For the death he died he died to sin, once for all, but the life he lives he lives to God. So, you also must consider yourselves dead to sin and alive to God in Christ Jesus."

Romans 6:1–10

I have always hated scary movies. I refuse to go to haunted houses or on haunted hayrides. Scary stuff just isn't my thing. I can't help but find this ironic, however, because Halloween is my favorite holiday of the whole year. Halloween is the one time of the year where anyone can be anything. Do you want to be your favorite superhero? Go ahead! Do you want to be an animal or live one night as your dream profession? Dress up! Do you want to be a clever play on words or an inside joke? Do it! Anyone can be anything on Halloween.

There is, however, one costume that always creeped me out a little more than most. I wasn't creeped out because it was a "scary" costume. I just always thought it was weird. Yep. I'm talking about zombie costumes. In essence, a zombie is a rotting, nasty, scary, dead but alive person. The concept of being alive but dead seems so weird to me. Either you are alive or you are dead, not both at the same time. A zombie seems to mix the two into a paradox. Most today refer to these characters as "the living dead." I assume the authors of the New Testament didn't know exactly what a zombie was, but they knew all too well the reality of being "the living dead."

In the previous chapter, we discussed at length the fact that human beings outside of Christ are spiritually dead. Paul makes this clear in Ephesians 2:1, "you were **dead** in your trespasses and sins." Jesus makes a similar statement when he describes the before and after state of the prodigal son in Luke 15:24. "For this my son was dead and is alive again." The prodigal son did not literally die. He was spiritually dead because he followed after his passions and lusts and because he rebelled against his father. In the same way, we are spiritually dead when we follow after our passions and lusts and rebel against God our father. The problem comes when we want to be alive in Christ but dead in our sins at the same time. I call this attitude "zombie faith."

Zombie faith is when someone claims to be a Christian but still lives a continually habitual sinful life. This person has been baptized but still engages in things that disgust God. Throughout this chapter, I want to explore three elements of zombie faith and give suggestions on how we can keep dead things buried for good.

What Was Buried?

Remember when you were baptized? You stepped one foot at a time into a body of water. You confessed your faith in Christ. You confessed him as Lord. You admitted that you are a sinner and that you need salvation. Then you were lowered completely into the water. Your whole body was buried under the water. Then you were lifted up from the water where you could breathe the breath of new life. Hopefully, you understood then that by burying your physical body in water, you were also putting to death your former spiritual self. The old man, as Paul often calls it, stays in the grave while the new man rises to live a life called of God.

But what exactly has been buried? What exactly have I put to death by the power of Christ? What is no longer a part of me? There are a few ways of answering this question. The first is to say that we put to death the former bad things that we have done. In other words, the sins that occurred prior to our baptism are no longer seen by God. This of course is true based on Paul's words in Rom 3:24–25. However, this does not satisfy the question to the fullest extent. The second is to say that we put to death any future sins we may want to commit. In other words, when we rise out of the water, we are making a pledge to never willfully sin again. This ideal is true based on the fact that Scripture teaches us to walk in the light (John 11:9; Eph 5:8; 1 John 1:7); yet, this does not satisfy the question fully. Another option is to say that we put to death all internal desires. That is, it is impossible to even be tempted by sin because we know the temptation is wrong. However, this view goes completely against Scripture. We know that Christians have their temptations. Even Jesus was tempted in all ways we are (Heb 2:18; 4:15). So, what then is it exactly that we put to death?

In a way, we put to death a combination of all that has been mentioned to this point. Yes, we put to death our desire for sin. Yes, God marks out our former sins. Yes, we try daily to put to death our temptation at the root of their source, but it is still more than that. Maybe Paul can answer it better. He writes, "We know that our old self was crucified with him in order that the body of sin might be brought to nothing, so that we would no longer be enslaved to sin." Why did we spiritually die? Paul says we died in order that we would no longer be slaves of sin. It is important that we understand what Paul is saying here. Slavery in the 1st century was different than what we think of within our own modern history. While the two certainly have their differences, one thing still remains the same. Slavery implies two things: (1) you are to be fully obedient to your master and

(2) you do not own yourself. Slavery was just as common in Paul's day as driving a car is in our own day. It is commonly believed that slaves outnumbered free Roman citizens 3 to 1 in Rome itself. The audience of Paul's letter (i.e., the Roman Christians) knew well what it meant to be a slave. They understood what it meant to be the physical property of someone else. Many of them may have been slaves. Therefore, when Paul says that we put to death the old self so that we may no longer be slaves of sin, he is in essence saying the only way to have true freedom is to put the old self to death. So, what is buried? The old self is also called "the flesh" or "things of the flesh" throughout the New Testament. What then do these things entail? Notice what Paul says in Galatians 5:19–21. "Now the works of the flesh are evident: sexual immorality, impurity, sensuality, idolatry, sorcery, enmity, strife, jealousy, fits of anger, rivalries, dissensions, divisions, envy, drunkenness, orgies, and things like these. I warn you, as I warned you before, that those who do such things will not inherit the kingdom of God." Paul goes on to say that those who have been crucified with Christ have put these things to death (Gal 5:24). Here's what we bury. We bury anything that has something to do with our former separation from God.

Why Raise Dead Things?

Why do we desire to walk around as a new person but still drag the casket alongside ourselves? Why do we exist as the living dead? This is a difficult question to answer. Honestly, I do not know that I will answer it in full. However, my goal remains the same as it always is. I hope to give you just enough information here to ignite a spark in your mind that will hopefully aid you in learning more about your walk with the Lord.

Sometimes we neglect to realize that Christians still sin. The apostle John knew this well when he wrote his first letter. The whole book of 1 John (in my opinion) is written with the simple theme "know that you know that you know." In other words, the purpose of 1 John is to help the Christian know firmly that Jesus is the messiah and that we have salvation through him and only him. It really bothers me when I hear members of the body of Christ say things like, "You'll go to hell if you think a bad thought," or, "If you don't ask God to forgive you for every single sin you have committed, then you're not truly saved." 1 John completely throws those ideas in the garbage. John writes, "If we say we have no sin, we deceive ourselves, and the truth is not in us. If we confess our sins, he is faithful and just to forgive us our sins and to cleanse us from all unrighteousness. If we say we have not sinned, we make him a liar, and his word is not in us" (1 John 1:8–10). Ultimately, John is admitting that everyone sins—Christian or non-Christian alike. The difference, however, is Jesus. For the Christian, Jesus is there when we fall. I want to be clear that this is not an excuse to willfully sin. Notice 1 John 1:7, "If we walk in the light as he is in the light, we have fellowship with one another and the blood of Jesus cleanses us from all sin." This is a conditional sentence marked by the word "if." The second half of the sentence is only true *if* the first half of the sentence is kept. Therefore, we must be walking in the light in order for his blood to cleanse us. That being said, it is possible to walk in the light and stumble. This verse promises that, as long as we are repentant, Jesus's blood not only washes away the sins that were committed before our baptism but continues to keep our souls cleansed from the stain of sin.

So, it is true that Christians still sin even though we do not want to do so. The problem is our willingness to repent every single day. When Peter told the crowd on the day of Pentecost what they must do, his first command was not to be baptized but to **repent**. The problem is that most of us do not want to live in continual repentance. This is why we "carry the casket." We can be the "new man" around everyone else but when we are alone, we can break out the old man even though he is supposed to be dead and buried.

Dead things stink. I was blessed to live on a farm for the majority of my life. We raised cattle, horses, sheep, goats, pigs, and chickens at one time or another. I loved all these animals—except the chickens. I hated the chickens. It was common on the farm to have an animal die due to sickness or even to be killed by a coyote. It often fell my lot to take the dead animal to a small area by a little creek that lie in the back of a field on our property. There the animal would eventually be eaten by buzzards and would ultimately decompose into compost. Once the animal died, it didn't take long for that animal to start stinking. You could smell the animal all the way across our thirty-three-acre farm. Even though you couldn't see the animal, it was evident that there was something dead around. After seeing and smelling the dead animal, one might wonder, "Why would anyone want to be around something like this?" The same could be asked about the "Christian" who lives a life of continual sin.

There are some good examples of this found within the text of Scripture. The first that comes to my mind are the Christians in Corinth. When Paul begins his first letter to the Corinthian church, he addresses it to the church of God in Corinth, to those sanctified in Christ Jesus, and to those called to be saints (1 Cor 1:2). In other words, Paul is making it clear that the recipients of his letter have been baptized and are counted as saved Christians—part of the body of Christ. However, it does not take very long (only 8 verses later) for Paul to address the first of several problems the church was facing along with sins the church was committing. The church was divided, the church was abusing the Lord's supper, the church was engaging in idolatry, and even certain members were committing horrible sexual sins. This was a "zombie" church. They were made alive in Christ when they were added to his body, but they were still spiritually dead.

Fortunately, they had Paul—a man who was willing to help them live as true Christians. It is clear that Paul obviously had a great love for this congregation. It is that great love that prompted such a disciplinary letter. It may be that you have been baptized into Christ but you are still living a life of sin. Please don't get upset when someone tells you that they are concerned about your soul. We are called to look out for one another. We are to be each other's spiritual keepers. Paul knew this well. His words of discipline are rooted in love. So too must our words be rooted in love.

So, what should we do once we realize that we are dragging this dead person along with us? How do we stop living a "zombie faith" and start living in the blessing of eternal life given by God? More of this will be discussed in the next subsection, but it is important to give one quick example here.

This man was called a man after God's own heart. This man was a valiant warrior. This man was chosen to be king over God's people. You guessed it. This man was David. You probably know his story well, but if you do not, I strongly encourage you to read his story in full. David was a godly man who was tempted by ungodly things. In 2 Samuel 11:1, the Bible says that all the kings went out to battle, but David stayed in Jerusalem. We should know already that something is wrong. David is a king. Why is he not out fighting with his soldiers? It just doesn't make sense. Regardless of why he didn't go with them into battle, we know that his stay at Jerusalem was going to cause a huge problem. The text goes on to say that in the late afternoon, David saw a beautiful woman bathing on her roof. David was so smitten by this woman that he sent for her because he wanted to have a sexual relationship with her. This ultimately caused the woman to become pregnant. What I haven't told you yet is that this woman was married to a Hittite man named Uriah, one of David's leading soldiers. (We know this because of the proximity of his home to David's palace.) Because she was a married woman and David was a married man, David had committed adultery himself while also forcing her to commit the same sin. As a result, David tried to cover up his crime which ultimately led to Uriah being killed in battle.

Though David was not the one who physically killed Uriah, David was nonetheless guilty of murder. What could he do? He had committed terrible sins that would forever impact his life and the lives of others. It seems that for David all hope of being a man after God's own heart had flown out of the window.

If you have never read the 51st psalm, I hope you will. Most biblical scholars believe this psalm was penned after David had committed these sins with Bathsheba (Uriah's wife). In essence, the psalm is a prayer that promises repentance and begs God for forgiveness. Notice verses 10–13.

> Create in me a clean heart, O God, and renew a right spirit within me. Cast me not away from your presence, and take not your Holy Spirit from me. Restore to me the joy of your salvation, and uphold me with a willing spirit. Then I will teach transgressors your ways, and sinners will return to you.

David admits that what he had done was wrong. He prays fervently for God to not only forgive him for what he has done, but for God to work in his spirit so that he will not fall to such temptation again. David does not seem to only want God to overlook his wrongdoing. He ultimately wants to live a life that is totally pleasing to God in every way—a life of continued repentance. Notice these words, "Restore to me the joy of your salvation." There is joy in salvation! It is a joy that cannot be found anywhere else. David's example proves that God can forgive and restore even the "zombiest" of our faiths.

How to Keep It Buried

This section might be the most difficult thing of which I will write in this book. We know that we are to put off the old man. In other words, we must live a totally changed life. We must keep our minds on things above and not on things of the earth. This is called *regeneration.*

The term *regeneration* is only used twice in all of Scripture. Both times are in the New Testament—once by Jesus in Matthew 19:28 and once by Paul in Titus 3:5. It is the Titus passage to which we must turn our attention.

> He saved us not by works of righteousness that we have done but on the basis of his mercy, through the washing of the new birth and the renewing of the Holy Spirit. (Titus 3:5)

Regeneration literally translated simply means "new birth." That is exactly what Jesus told Nicodemus that one must do in order to enter the kingdom of God (cf. John 3:3–8). Regeneration is an act of God that both rests on his involvement in our lives as well as our willingness to be obedient to his will alone. It is the means by which God imparts spiritual life to the believer.

If we understand ourselves at the time of our baptism to be "born of God," we must then agree that the birthing process is only something that can come from God. God can only give his own likeness. A horse, for example, always gives birth to a horse, a cow will always give birth to a cow, a dog will always give birth to a dog, and so on. Therefore, God will only be able to give new birth to his own attributes. For example, 1 Peter 1:21 says that when one is born again, he is born of "imperishable seed."

Regeneration is God the Father and God the Holy Spirit working within us. There are some who suggest this is accomplished by means of something that is irresistible. This is often called "irresistible grace." However, it is important to note that obedience is the key to any part of godliness. *Regeneration,* therefore, is only possible if you allow God to transform your heart (cf. Eph 2:10). The exact nature of regeneration is a mystery. We know that we were spiritually dead to God before our washing of regeneration (i.e., baptism) and now we are alive in Christ. If we are truly being regenerated, every part of our lives and our being must be impacted. Notice 2 Corinthians 5:17, "If anyone is in Christ, he is a new creation. The old has passed away. The new has come." The purpose of regeneration remains true nonetheless. It is God's spiritual awaking within the life of the believer.

Regeneration is both instantaneous and continual. Regeneration occurs instantly when one is raised from baptism. The soul is washed clean by the blood of Christ. It is at this point that regeneration must begin. From here on we are to live as living sacrifices, holy and acceptable to God (cf. Rom 12:1–2). Though we have been made right with God and it is as if our sins had never been committed, we are not completely morally perfect when we come out of the baptistry. We still must face the consequences of our past. We will still sin and fall short of the glory of God (cf. 1 John 1; Rom 3:23). Thus, *regeneration* is a lifelong process. One might call this process our "growth in sanctification" or "growing in the grace of Jesus." If one has truly been born again (i.e., truly regenerated) and one's baptism was not for show or arrogant desires, then there must be an evident change in one's life. So, how do we live a regenerated life? What are some ways in which we can know that God is actually working in us?

First, we must possess Christlike love. 1 John 4:7 says, "Beloved, let us love one another, for love is from God, and whoever loves has been born of God and knows God." This Christlike love is best defined (though other definitions could be added) as unconditional compassion. Love is not a feeling that you feel like you're feeling when you feel a feeling that you've never felt before (to borrow a quote from Keith Parker). Love is always denoted as an action. When Jesus looked at the crowds that followed him, he had compassion on them. He did not heal the sick only because they were sick. He did not feed the hungry only because they were hungry. He did these things because he had compassion on these people. What about you? When you see that lonely person at the lunch table, do you say "Hi!" or ask that person to sit with you? Do you have a desire to make life better for the people that are around you? Do you look at people and see helpless souls instead of inconveniences? Jesus did. Our goal is to always be like him.

Second, we must stop making habitual sin a regular occurrence in our lives. 1 John 5:18 says, "We know that everyone who has been born of God does not keep on sinning, but he who was born of God protects him, and the evil one does not touch him." There seems to be a paradox here. We know that Christians will sin from time to time. So, how do we just stop sinning? The point here is for the Christian to live a life where he intentionally attempts to not sin. We know what sin is. We know that sin separates us from God. Therefore, a regenerated life earnestly tries to "be perfect as our heavenly father is perfect" (Matt 5:48). This is an impossible task. Thankfully, God does not demand perfection. He does, however, demand progression—more on that later.

Being born of God means we have victory over the temptations of this world. 1 John 5:4 says, "For everyone who has been born of God overcomes the world. And this is the victory that has overcome the world—our faith." This world is a rough place. The longer you look, the more sin you see. This is largely due in today's society to the ideology of postmodernism. That may not mean much to you, but you're living in it; so, you should probably learn what *postmodernism* means. Postmodernism is a word that describes the time after the modern age marked by the cultural, intellectual, and technological advancements made in the 19th and 20th centuries. In other words, we live (at least at the time of this writing) in a post-modern age. *Postmodernism* is marked namely by the ideal that absolute truth does not exist. For Christians, this is terribly difficult because we believe God, Jesus, the Spirit, and the Scriptures all encompass absolute truth. While it is certainly difficult to live in this world, we have assurance that we have overcome the world because we are born of God. In other words, the world cannot conquer us.

That is not to say that we do not have a role in the process as well. We must practice self-discipline. As a newborn child of God, we have to change certain things about our life. We have to make a conscious decision to live for God every day. This requires a disciplined life. Self-discipline comes in a variety of forms. Some of us may practice self-discipline by not spending time with certain people who tempt us to sin. Others of us may find ourselves spending more time with these people in an attempt to show them Jesus. However, I would only recommend the latter if you are strong and mature enough in your walk with God to not be tempted by these people. It would be very easy for someone to be a greater influence on you than you are on them.

Self-discipline may be best illustrated by the practice of fasting. I was blessed to write my master's thesis on this topic when I was a graduate student at Freed-Hardeman University. After I graduated, I turned my research into a book called *Should Christians Fast: A Study of Contemporary Spirituality from Matthew 6:1–18.* When I first began thinking about fasting, I thought it was just a good idea for really pious people to do. However, the more I studied the practice in the life of Jesus and the early church, the more I realized that the act of fasting isn't just about going hungry. It is about disciplining your flesh to be more focused on spiritual matters. Fasting removes something physical from your life (i.e., food) so you can focus on spiritual things (e.g., prayer, your relationships, the Word, etc.). When you fast, you realize it is incredibly tempting to cheat. What I mean is that it is really tempting to take a small bite of food after a few hours or to say, "I'll go grab a Coke," even though you had committed to drink only water. Self-discipline is basically being able to tell yourself "No." If you want dead things to stay dead, you must train yourself to say no to the things that have been spiritually put to death. No one said this would be easy. Discipline implies hard work must be done. No one can make you refuse to do the things you once did—not even God. This is not because he doesn't possess the power to do so. It is because God will never force you to love him. If a man forced his wife to marry him, that would not be true love, would it? Love must be freely given and freely received. Therefore, only you can discipline yourself. It's not some magical or mystical thing that happens overnight. Self-discipline requires a lifetime of work.

We often only pray when we something bad happens. When a loved one gets sick or passes away, we go to God and ask for healing and comfort. When our significant other treats us negatively, we pray that God will soften their hearts. While these are certainly things that we must pray about, Paul seems to understand prayer as more than the giving of requests for supernatural intervention. Paul understands prayer to be a continual conversation with God—a conversation that never gets old. Paul tells the Thessalonian Christians in his first letter to that congregation to pray without ceasing (1 Thess 5:17). It is not that we are to pray for 24 hours each day. It means that we are to never cease from turning to God in times of joy and in times of sorrow. Because God is our father, he will never turn a deaf ear to our cries.

I think, too, we have forgotten how to pray during times when things are good. When Paul addresses Timothy, Philemon, the Corinthian church, and the Philippian church, he states that he thanks God in his prayers for them. I've often wondered what Paul's prayers sounded like. They must have taken forever to say. Paul constantly writes that he prayed for all the congregations of Christians as well as specific individuals. Further, Paul spent a great deal of time praying for his own needs. However, I don't think we can ignore the fact that Paul knew exactly how to pray a prayer of thanksgiving. When was the last time you told God how thankful you are for your material blessings, your friends, your family, and especially your salvation?

Remember how we said walking in the light and following after God is a huge struggle? Have you ever experienced something that was really hard, but then you asked for help, and the task became easier? I remember when I was starting my college career as a Bible major at Freed-Hardeman University way back in the fall of 2011. I knew I wanted to preach, but I didn't know Greek or Hebrew, I didn't know all the prophecies of Jesus, and to be completely honest, I probably couldn't have listed all the books of the Bible in their correct order. I remember sitting in my Basics of Biblical Greek class staring at my textbook not knowing an alpha (A, α) from a gamma (Γ, γ). (By the way, alpha is the first letter of the Greek alphabet. Gamma is the third.) What was I to do? I wanted to be successful in the class. I definitely didn't want to look dumb. So, after receiving horrible grades on my quizzes and tests, I finally went to my professor and asked for extra tutoring. Thankfully he was willing to help me out. As a result, I was able to make A's in every Greek class I took from then onward.

God works in a similar way. He is always there to help, but we must be humble enough to ask. We need to realize, however, that God isn't going to wave his magic wand and make everything perfect for us overnight. In the same way that my professor forced me to do extra assignments and spend more hours with him and a textbook, God wants us to spend more time with him and his word. If we are going to keep dead things buried, we must be willing to talk to God no matter the circumstances. We must be willing to thank God in the good times and lean on him in the bad times.

When walking the new journey of a Christian, it is imperative that you surround yourself with likeminded people. In other words, you need to seek out opportunities to spend time with the people of God. In the 1st century, it was illegal to worship any gods other than the gods of the state. Because of this, the early Christians were seen as outlaws and enemies of the Roman government. In addition to these things, the people of the 1st century believed that when something bad happened (e.g., a volcano, flood, a bad economy, illness, death, etc.), it was because the gods were not being properly appeased. Therefore, people in the 1st century often blamed Christians for the bad things happening in the world. Imagine living in this type of world. Christians were literally hated and cut off from the rest of society. All they had were each other.

We call each other "brother" and "sister" for a reason. In Christ, we are heirs to the promise of God. God is our father. Jesus is our brother. We are the family of God. In the 1st century, the church was completely cut off from their former way of life. Businesses that were operated by Christians suffered because no one would do business with these criminals. Families were divided because some chose to follow God while others chose to follow Caesar or Zeus. The words of Jesus ring ever true here when he said, "If anyone comes to me and does not hate his own father and mother and wife and children and brothers and sisters, yes, and even his own life, he cannot be my disciple" (Luke 14:26). No, Jesus is not saying to *hate* your family in the sense that one should despise his family or hold ill will toward them. Rather, Jesus is saying that he must be first in our lives above all others. Being a disciple of Jesus can very literally mean giving up everything else in order to follow Jesus.

This is why you need Christian friends. I don't mean friends who just go to church on Sunday morning. I mean true Christian friends. It is not uncommon in congregations today for many people (especially young people) to have "church friends." What I mean is that most young Christians have friends that they see from time to time at church, but that's the extent of their relationship. While these relationships are great and should be commended, I think we all need more than that. I want to encourage you, if you are able, to make a few (or more than a few) **REAL** Christian friends. These are friends that you call when your world is tumbling upside down. These are the people who stand beside you on your wedding day or come to the hospital when your babies are born. These are people who—in every sense of the word—are your brothers and sisters in Christ. Who knows, you may end up marrying one of them. I did.

I tell kids in my congregation on a regular basis that they desperately need to adopt a church grandparent. This is not to discredit their own biological grandparents, but it does stress the value of intergenerational relationships. One of the biggest challenges facing the church today is the issue of division. The church is divided because congregations are divided. Unfortunately, so many congregations are divided because of the different point of views between the older and younger generations. While this issue is something the church desperately needs to fix, the point of having an adopted church grandparent goes far beyond the issue of unity.

An adopted church grandparent should function the exact same way your own grandparent would function in your life. You should speak to this person on a regular basis. You should spend time with this person outside of the worship assembly. You should be invited to this person's home. You should invite this person to your home. You should have this person's phone number on speed-dial. You should not be afraid to call this person at any time of the day for any reason.

When I was growing up in church, I had several people who I considered to be my adopted church grandparents, so much so that I still refer to one such couple as Memaw and Granddaddy. These were the people who helped me out in the roughest of times. The great thing about older people is that they have been where you are now. They can look back at their life and teach you lessons that you have likely not learned yet.

The man I referred to as "Granddaddy" is a great example of this. He and I shared a great love for horseback riding and showing horses in local shows. There would be some afternoons where I would go to Memaw and Granddaddy's, ride my horse for a bit, get critiqued, ride some more, help feed and water the animals, then go home to do schoolwork. I recall attempting to ride a mare that had a little bit of a temper. Well, let's say she was high-strung. I recall that day the sun was shining and the temperature was quite comfortable. I just knew this mare was going to be a handful. The good weather made her feel good. When she felt good, she felt spunky. After spending what seemed like hours warming her up (or wearing her down), I was finally able to hop on and ride. I put my foot in the stirrup, climbed on her back, and away we went.

When practicing for a horse show, it is best to ride in a round-pen. This is basically a makeshift arena constructed from panels that are set up in the shape of a circle or oval. The exhibitor would ride the horse in one direction in three different gaits (flat walk, running walk, and canter), then the exhibitor would turn his horse and do the same thing in the other direction. It seems simple enough. However, there is only a few inches at best between your leg and the panels. This particular mare loved being close to the panels and would often bump my leg against them. Granddaddy saw that this was happening, but it wasn't the horse's fault. Granddaddy told me that my feet were pointing outward from the stirrup. This was forcing my toes to catch the rail and hurt my feet and legs. He caught that mistake, taught me how to fix it, and I became a better rider and exhibitor because of it. I know this little story isn't discussing some big sin or terrible temptation, but it just goes to show how beneficial it is to have an older, wiser set of eyes watching out for your life.

One more thing before we move on to the next suggestion: be careful about who you choose to fill this role. Not every "older person" is fit to be a "grandparent" in the way that I am speaking. There are a lot of older people who are overly critical of the younger generations. To be fair, the younger generations need some harsh criticism at times, but this person—for the purpose of helping you get to Heaven—needs to be someone who can respond in love to your faults and encourage you in your successes.

One last thing…go to church! Make a habit of assembling with the saints every time the opportunity arises. As I sit at my computer typing out these words, I am mindful of the world in which I live. Perhaps these words will far exceed my own life...I hope they do. However, I hope even more so that the culture of the world that is to come after I am gone will be better in some sense than it is now. Yet, even beyond that I pray that the dedication of youth and young adults to the church is far greater than it is in my lifetime. Young people ages 35 and younger are rapidly leaving the church in growing numbers. They are not leaving one congregation in search for another. They are leaving the church, their faith, and their salvation behind. This mass exodus from the church is the product of several causes, not least is the inability of church members to nurture and love those who are younger.

This may be a stretch for some of you, but imagine you have been away from your spouse for a week on business. The whole time you were away, you were writing reports for work, making sure others are taken care of, and preparing for meeting after meeting. You've only been able to talk to your spouse on the phone for a few minutes, though not every night. All you want to do is spend true, quality time with your spouse.

Finally, you are able to return home. You pull into the driveway barely able to keep your eyes open from exhaustion. You see your spouse through the window waiting for your arrival. However, the plane ride has you struggling to stay awake, the food you ate for supper is slowly digesting in your stomach, and the radio station is lulling you toward intense drowsiness. You turn off the car, sit in the spot for a few moments longer, take a deep breath, and finally walk into your home.

Your spouse meets you at the door with a hug and kiss thankful that you made it back safely. Your spouse says, "Let me tell you about what I have been up to these past few days." You both go to the couch where you take your place in your favorite spot. As your spouse begins to explain everything you need to know, you get up and drive off to your buddy's house. Even though you're tired, you'd rather spend time with a friend than spend time with your spouse.

Does this show your undying love to your spouse? Of course not. You're not there. You are ignoring the need of the one you love and the one who loves you by removing yourself from the setting. We do this same thing when we refuse to come to church. In essence, what you are saying to the almighty, sovereign, good, and just creator of the universe is, "I know you're important. I know you want to spend time with me, but I don't want to spend time with you." If we don't want to spend time with God now, why would we want to spend an eternity with him in Heaven? Devotion to God must be the product of our whole heart (Deut 6:4–5).

The whole purpose of gathering on the first day of the week is to worship the true and living God in whom we live and move and have our being (Acts 17:28). God is certainly worthy of worship. Worship is how we show God that we love him. We praise him in song. We remember the death of Christ with the Lord's Supper. We study his word, pray, and give. All of these things allow an avenue for us to show God that we love him in our own love language.

Love, by definition, must be freely given AND freely received. If a man were to kidnap a woman and said, "I love you, so I'm going to keep you tied to this wall forever," the woman would clearly understand there is no true love in the scenario at all. The man is forcing himself on the woman. That is not love. That is oppression. The same is true with God. God will never force you to love him or to express your love for him because if he did, it would not truly be *love*. God will never force you to worship. He wants you to worship simply because you love him. When you miss worship, you miss your date with God. Imagine how your significant other would feel if you purposefully missed a very special date. God always desires an intimate expression of love from each of us.

Hebrews 10:24–25 says this, "And let us consider how to stir up one another to love and good works, not neglecting to meet together, as is the habit of some, but encouraging one another, and all the more as you see the Day drawing near." Verse 24 illustrates what we are to do when we are gathered in the worship assembly. We are to "stir up one another to love and good works." How? By not neglecting the assembling of ourselves together. What do we do when we assemble? We encourage one another. We build each other up. We edify each other. This is why it is vital that you not only find a church family that serves and worships God in a way that aligns perfectly with Scripture, but also that you make a habit of attending these meetings whenever they happen. That is how we keep dead things buried. Being a Christian was never something intended to be performed alone. (For more, see the appendix.)

Personal Reflection

1. What sins are you having trouble keeping dead?
2. Who are three people you can lean on when you are struggling with sin?
3. Are you friends with Christian people?
4. Is attending worship services a habit in your life?
5. What are some other things you could do to live a life of regeneration and repentance?

"Finally, be strong in the Lord and in the strength of his might. Put on the whole armor of God, that you may be able to stand against the schemes of the devil. For we do not wrestle against flesh and blood, but against the rulers, against the authorities, against the cosmic powers over this present darkness, against the spiritual forces of evil in the heavenly places. Therefore, take up the whole armor of God, that you may be able to withstand in the evil day, and having done all, to stand firm. Stand therefore, having fastened on the **belt of truth**, and having put on the **breastplate of righteousness**, and, as **shoes for your feet, having put on the readiness given by the gospel of peace**. In all circumstances take up the **shield of faith**, with which you can extinguish all the flaming darts of the evil one; and t**ake the helmet of salvation**, and the **sword of the Spirit**, which is the word of God, praying at all times in the Spirit, with all prayer and supplication. To that end, keep alert with all perseverance, making supplication for all the saints, and also for me, that words may be given to me in opening my mouth boldly to proclaim the mystery of the gospel, for which I am an ambassador in chains, that I may declare it boldly, as I ought to speak."

Ephesians 6:10–20

"I desire then that in every place the men should pray, lifting holy hands without anger or quarreling; likewise, also that women should adorn themselves in respectable apparel, with modesty and self-control, not with braided hair and gold or pearls or costly attire, but with what is proper for women who profess godliness—with good works."

1 Timothy 2:8–10

I have to admit it—farm life is a fun life. I love being outside. Honestly, I love good, hard work. That may seem insane, but I really enjoy working hard because when all is said and done, I can look back, see the progress I have made, and consider it a job well done. It allows me to be proud of my accomplishments. Living on a farm taught me this great life lesson. Living on a farm also taught me that something really simple could be made unnecessarily complicated by things you would never consider. Take feeding the cows for example. My morning routine as a teenager was simple and straightforward: wake up, put on my "barn clothes," walk to the barn, feed the animals (mostly the cows and pigs), get the tractor running, put out a bale of hay, put the tractor back in the shed, go to the house, get cleaned up, eat a small bite of breakfast, and head off to school by 7:30 AM. No big deal, right?

Now imagine the same routine, but the temperature is 20° F. In Tennessee, the temperature could be 75° on Tuesday and 25° on Wednesday. The weather here is insanely difficult to predict. Anyways, let's say it's now 20° outside. You know it is 20° but you're a tough ole boy (or gal), so you don't grab your thick, warm jacket. You *believe* the jacket will keep you safe from the elements, but you neglect to wear it. Do you think you will be warm without it?

My dad used to use this illustration all the time to show how Jesus works in our lives. Many people think that as long as they *believe* in Jesus, then he will save them from the wrath of God. However, this cannot be true. James says that even the demons believe and shudder (Jas 2:19). In fact, a demon was the first to address Jesus as the son of God (Mark 3:11, 5:7; Luke 4:3). Are the demons saved? No. In fact that is made explicitly clear in 2 Pet 2:4.

> "[But] God did not spare the angels when they sinned…"

Yes, believing in God and believing in Jesus is vital to one's salvific process. One must *believe* if one is to be saved. However, belief, as we think of it, cannot be enough. In the ancient world, for one to *believe* meant that one's actions would be the direct result of this belief.

I do not know who originated this story (I've been told it is a true story), but it proves a significant point here. There was once a man who was a tightrope walker for a circus. In his act, he would walk from one end of the rope to the other with his balancing aid, then he would drop the balancing aid, walk back across the rope, grab a wheelbarrow, and push the wheelbarrow across the tightrope to the other side. Being the daredevil that he was, this performer decided he would take his act to Niagara Falls. The tightrope was stretched across the falls and the man walked from one end to the other, grabbed his wheelbarrow and walked back to the other side. While the crowd was cheering, the performer asked if the audience *believed* he could do it again. Of course, having seen the act completed in its perfection, the crowd responded with a resounding, "Yes!" The performer then asked, "Do you believe I could do it with something in the wheelbarrow?" The crowd's response was again a resounding, "Yes!" The performer paused for a moment and asked, "So, which one of you wants to get in the wheelbarrow?"

In the ancient world, belief was matched with action. This is why James can say, "Faith without works is dead" (Jas 2:26). When you were baptized into Christ, you were putting your belief into action. In essence, you were putting on the coat (i.e., Jesus) before going to the freezing outdoors (i.e., into the sinful world). This is exactly what Paul says in Galatians 3:27. "For as many of you as have been baptized into Christ Jesus have *put on* Christ." The Greek word translated "put on" literally means "to wear." We wear Christ! We have discussed this verse in previous chapters and will no doubt bring it up again as we move forward. Thus, I do not wish to explore this verse in particular. Rather, I want to ask the question: what does "wearing Jesus" look like?

We all have brands that we like to wear and represent. I poke fun at my younger brother-in-law sometimes because he calls himself a "brand boy." In other words, he will only wear name brand clothing. Sometimes, he even refuses to mix brands. Basically, this means if he is wearing Nike shoes, then he must also wear Nike socks, Nike pants, and a Nike shirt. While I may laugh at him on occasion for his peculiarity with certain brands, being a Christian is really no different. If we are "wearing Jesus" then we cannot be wearing anything else. Though we will discuss the armor of God later, I want to first discuss the Christian's wardrobe in a more culturally modern way.

As a farm kid, I always wore either a cowboy hat (my personal favorite) or a baseball cap (usually with an agricultural reference or our farm name stamped on it). When people looked at my hat, they were able to learn a great deal about me. They knew to some extent what was on my mind. So, let's start at the top and work our way down. What goes on our head? Our head is what dictates every other part of our body. Jesus is called the "head of the church" in Colossians 1:18 because he is the leader and controller of his body. He is the "brain of the operation." Our head needs to be like his. I am not suggesting, however, that we think of ourselves as the leader of the church or even of our own lives. That goes completely against Matthew 16:24–26. However, Paul tells us to have the mind of Christ (Phil 2:5–8). This entails many different things, but two are important to note here.

First, this means being humble. Humility is being willing to count others as more important that yourself. To humble oneself literally means "to make low." The Greek word for "humble" paints the picture of a mountain being totally disintegrated. That's powerful stuff. Second, we must "set our minds on things above" (Col 3:2–4). Most of the time when we say, "That person has his head in the clouds," we mean it in a derogative way. We are usually saying that person is out of touch with reality or that one sees oneself as better than other people. Yet, Paul tells us that we are to set our minds on things above. In other words, our minds should be constantly set on Jesus, God, the Spirit, and other spiritual things.

I bet you think we're about to discuss the shirt/blouse/upper body covering next. Nope. No outfit is complete without sunglasses. So, what goes over our eyes when we are in Christ? Glasses, be they sunglasses or eyeglasses, are nothing more than a lens that allows the wearer to view the world more clearly and comfortably. In Christ, we see the world for what it is: a passing reality. As such, we are responsible for the things we look at. While his words were written hundreds of years before Jesus, the proverb writer gives great guidance when he says, "Let your eyes look directly forward, and your gaze be straight before you" (Prov 4:25). Don't be afraid to see the world through the lens of Jesus.

Now, we can focus on the shirt. This may not be true for everyone, but it seems that usually the whole outfit revolves around the shirt. Whatever color or pattern the shirt is will impact the remainder of the outfit. Thus, the love of God will act in this capacity. The love of God must dictate everything we do. Even Jesus said, "By this all people will know you are my disciples, that you love one another" (John 13:35). When we learn how to love with a godly love, everything else we do (i.e., where we go, what we say, what we do, and how we think) will be the result of this love.

The style or type of pants to wear seems to be an afterthought for me. I know this is more difficult for you female readers, but my pants go with everything. I have pants that are matched to suits, sports coats, or just a plain T-shirt. The pants are necessary to complete the outfit, but they don't really (at least for me) dictate the outfit. Usually, they aren't the first thing to be noticed. Honestly, if someone notices your pants first, you might want to change your outfit. So, the pants represent a fundamental part of the ensemble but not to the point that it is overbearing. This, I think, represents our time in private study.

Yes, we need to study the Bible. In the same way that pants provide a place to hold our important things (e.g., pockets for a wallet, phone, pocket knife, etc.), so too does our study get tucked away in our own understanding. The things we study are for us alone. Sure, others can see what we have studied when the instance arises. However, we should never use our knowledge in a forceful in-your-face kind of way.

Though we might be tempted to move straight into a discussion of the "shoes" as Paul did, there are two more things to consider. I love socks. I used to be that kid that hated getting socks for Christmas or for my birthday; but now, I love it! I especially love socks with funny designs on them. I have socks with coffee cups, sharks, gingerbread men, and even Santa riding a sled saying, "Sleigh all day." But no matter how cool your socks are, it always ruins your day when your sock gets wet. I can tolerate just about anything except a wet sock or a pebble in my shoe. Honestly, I am uncomfortable even writing about it. The Christian's sock represents his or her surroundings. When things are godly, moral, and holy, then we should feel comfortable. When things are ungodly, immoral, or unholy, we should feel just as uncomfortable as when we have a wet sock.

Growing up on the farm meant constantly being on your feet. It also meant other things might be on your feet as well. I can recall showing cattle in my time as a high-schooler. The animal would be led into the show ring by the exhibitor who paraded himself in front of or beside the animal. It seems simple, but a good exhibitor would know that he must move his legs and feet in the exact same time and pattern as his animal. If the cow moved his left leg then his front leg, the exhibitor was to follow suit. This makes you and the animal look better to the judge. Even so, if one does not move in this way, one runs a greater risk of having his foot smooshed under the weight of the animal. One could always tell an inexperienced exhibitor because he or she would be wearing steel-toed boots. These boots were worn in an effort to keep one's toes from being trampled under the weight of the animal right beside him. Being a Christian means that we might have our toes stepped on at one time or another. The "shoes" we wear do not imply we will never have our toes stepped on. They just help protect us when it happens. You will be made fun of for being a Christian. You will be refused service, not awarded a promotion, and have relationships end all because of your faith. It really hurts when that happens, but Jesus is worth it. Just because it hurts does not mean it has to be a fatal blow.

While it may seem that we have covered the complete ensemble (perhaps even more than you might have thought), there is still one more thing to discuss. Men do not give this much thought, though perhaps we should. Women on the other hand could not live without them. I am going to call this thing by its categorical name—accessories. Men wear wristwatches because it makes them look more professional. Ladies wear earrings and necklaces to enhance their appearance. Both men and women wear rings to signify their marital status. Accessories are a necessity to complete any outfit. Accessories are the small things that enhance your wardrobe. So, what small things can enhance your relationship with Jesus? This is somewhat of a loaded question because the things I am going to mention are not small at all. Rather, they are things the Christian does perhaps as more of an enhancement to his life rather than a true "doctrine" of faith. Prayer is significantly important in the life of a Christian, but *what we pray for* is (to a degree) left up to us to decide. Therefore, I want to challenge you to accessorize your Christianity by praying for your enemies. Accessories are small things that make a bold statement. Praying for someone you have a difficult time liking or being around is a seemingly small thing that will make a bold statement. Jesus commands his followers to love their enemies and pray for those who persecute them (Matt 5:44). Let this little accessory be evident in your wardrobe then move on to something else—perhaps volunteering for a church event or making food for a sick Christian. It may not seem like much but without it your wardrobe will be missing something vital.

The Whole Armor of God

The Christian's wardrobe goes beyond that of simply "looking" like a Christian. When Paul describes what a Christian should wear, he does not do so in the way one might expect. Paul does not describe anything casual. Instead, Paul describes something with which his audience would have been all too familiar. Paul likens the Christian wardrobe to armor. But why would Paul do this? Aren't Christians supposed to be peaceful people? Isn't peace part of the fruit of the Spirit? It doesn't seem to make sense that followers of Jesus would need armor.

The 1st century world that Paul was living in was a world of political uncertainty. Emperors would come and go seemingly overnight. Each emperor sought to expand the empire by means of warfare. In addition to expanding the empire geographically, the empire also needed to be monitored from the inside. Rumors of riots and uprisings were the norm in Rome and Roman provinces. Thus, Roman soldiers were just as common to see as were the clouds in the sky. When Paul describes the armor of God, he is not describing the armor of a medieval knight. Roman armor was built for the attack, not protection. The legs and arms of soldier were entirely vulnerable. The soldier only had a small shield and a little breastplate and helmet used to protect himself.

Roman Soldier

Paul begins by telling his readers what the purpose of the armor of God is. The armor of God is composed of six different components. Each component aids the Christian in fighting his spiritual battles. While we may think of "spiritual battles" as battles against temptation and sin, Paul describes spiritual warfare in another way.

Paul says, "Put on the whole armor of God, that you may be able to **stand against the schemes of the devil**. For we do not wrestle against flesh and blood, but **against the rulers**, against **authorities**, against **the cosmic powers over this present darkness**, against the **spiritual forces of evil in the heavenly places**" (Eph 6:11–12; emphasis added). Paul does not say that we are fighting a war against temptation or against our own sinful lives. That war has already been won in Jesus Christ. Yet, there is still a war to be fought. Unfortunately, Christians today do not seem to believe in the power of the devil. They think of the devil as just another bad bedtime story. He is interpreted as the mystic spirit of evil, not a real being. Dear reader, please know the devil is alive and active. Paul calls him the "prince of the power of the air" in Ephesians 2:2. He is not king over God's people, but he is the prince of this world.

We have a battle to fight against the devil. I suppose most of us already knew that. But what of our battle against the ruling authorities? Think back to Paul's day. The people in power were causing many problems for Christians. It was illegal to be a Christian in the 1st century. Christians were arrested and killed because they did not worship the gods of the state or the emperor. Take Roman coins for example. Roman coins were not very different from our coins today. They bore the image of the emperor with an inscription that circled the coin. The inscription would have the name of the emperor with a phrase of divinity. Sometimes the emperor would be called the "son of god" while other times he would just be given the title "divine." Everyone was supposed to worship the emperor. Christians, however, would never do such a thing. Because of the Christian's devotion to Jesus as the son of God and the truly divine one, many Christians were killed for their faith.

"Divine Augustus, Father [of Rome]"
Coin ca. 22 A. D. (during the reign of Tiberius) to honor Augustus

How would we respond if our government said that we could not worship or serve God anymore? Would be stop being Christians knowing we could go to jail or die for our faith? The early Christians were so devoted to the Lord that they refused to worship the emperor or false gods even though their lives were at stake.

Around 112 A. D., a man named Pliny the Younger wrote a letter to Trajan, the current emperor of Rome, about the problems that Christians were causing. Notice part of what he says:

> Meanwhile, in the case of those who were denounced to me as Christians, I have followed the following procedure: I interrogated them as to whether they were Christians; those who confessed I interrogated a second and a third time, threatening them with

punishment; those who persisted I ordered executed. For I had no doubt that, whatever the nature of their creed, stubbornness and inflexible obstinacy surely deserve to be punished. There were others possessed of the same folly; but because they were Roman citizens, I signed an order for them to be transferred to Rome.

Trajan's response is as follows:

You observed proper procedure, my dear Pliny, in sifting the cases of those who had been denounced to you as Christians. For it is not possible to lay down any general rule to serve as a kind of fixed standard. They are not to be sought out; if they are denounced and proved guilty, they are to be punished, with this reservation, that whoever denies that he is a Christian and really proves it — that is, by worshiping our gods — even though he was under suspicion in the past, shall obtain pardon through repentance. But anonymously posted accusations ought to have no place in any prosecution. For this is both a dangerous kind of precedent and out of keeping with the spirit of our age.

We are at war with the evil in this world. This evil is the result of Satan and manifested by authorities and powers. This is the great paradox of spiritual warfare: the war has been won in Christ, so we must fight every day.

Paul begins with the article of armor that is sported in the middle of the soldier. The purpose of a belt is to hold all the other articles of armor together. Without the belt, the breastplate will not be fastened nor would the sword have a place to be sheathed. The belt is necessary to hold the entire ensemble together in a way that is designed for each piece to be at its most functional. So, what holds our armor together? Truth does. Everything about Jesus, the gospel, the church, God, and his word rests on the foundation of truth. Unfortunately, many Christians act like Pilate did when Jesus was on trial. Jesus told Pilate that he came to bear witness to the truth. Confused, Pilate asked Jesus, "What is truth?" (John 18:37–38). Jesus had answered this question just a few chapters earlier in John's Gospel. In John 14:6, Jesus said to his disciples, "I am the way, the

truth, and the life." Everything about the Christian life must be rooted and tied up in Jesus.

The word "truth" occurs 141 times in the English Standard Version and 225 times in the American Standard Version. In other words, this word is kind of a big deal in the Bible. Truth is such a big deal that Scripture makes departing from the truth one of the most detrimental things a person could do.

The next item mentioned is the breastplate of righteousness. The breastplate was the metal guard that lay over a soldier's chest. The purpose of the breastplate was to protect the vital organs of the soldier in battle. The soldier may survive a laceration from a sword or spear on his leg, but he would not survive a blow to his heart or lungs. The breastplate may well have been the most important defensive mechanism for the soldier. If his shield was lost in battle, he would still be protected from piercing blows (to a degree of course).

What protects our heart? Paul says it is the breastplate of *righteousness*. When one thinks of the term *righteous* one likely thinks of being right or being good (i.e., being morally acceptable). However, as we learned in the first chapter, God is the one who imputes righteousness on those who are obedient to him. The righteousness of God is given to all who believe (Rom 3:22). Does this mean that Jesus gives me a slice of his righteousness? No, not at all. Righteousness is something I can have *because* of Jesus, not something I take *from* Jesus.

Righteousness is a gift only received in Christ. It comes as a result of doing the will of God. Note 1 John 3:7, "My little children, let no man lead you astray: he that does righteousness is righteous, even as he is righteous." But how does one *do* righteousness? In the late 1990s and early 2000s, it was a popular fashion statement for Christians to wear bracelets with the acronym WWJD. This stood for "What Would Jesus Do?" When one was faced with a dilemma or temptation, one was to look at that bracelet and ask "What would Jesus do?" *Doing righteousness* works in a similar way. Doing righteousness means more than doing good things or being a good person. It means being the living embodiment of Jesus on Earth. When people see you, they should see Jesus. That is what being "clothed in Christ" means.

Next, Paul discusses perhaps the least thought about aspect of the armor of God. Admittedly, it is difficult for us to understand this item in the way Paul means it here. He says, "…and as shoes for your feet, having put on the readiness given by the gospel of peace." The KJV puts it this way: "having shod your feet with the preparation of the gospel of peace."

There are two ways of interpreting this passage. Both are equally valid. The term "shod" refers to a horse whose hooves have been trimmed and given horseshoes. This would aid the horse in his ability to stand firm in the midst of battle. The same is true with the soldier. While most soldiers had only sandals for battle shoes, it was vital that they be able to stand with firm footing. The Romans were battle geniuses. When they engaged their enemies, they did so by arranging their soldiers in rows with their shields forming a fort-like protection over them (see picture below). This is called a phalanx formation.

Roman Soldiers in Battle Formation

The force of a whole other army is pushing on your formation. Without firm footing, the soldier could fall and cause the whole squadron to fail. In addition to this formation, the soldier would often be required to break from the cover of a shield to engage in hand to hand combat. Without proper footing, any little mistake could be devastating. With one slip, the soldier is vulnerable.

What are our feet firmly placed upon? Paul says our firm footing is on the preparation of the gospel of peace. That's a mouthful. It seems like there are so many parts to this construct that one's foot isn't rooted in just one thing but a plethora of things. In a way, that is true. However, the shoes that provide our firm footing in life are not placed in various different spots but in one unified theme. Let's take the construct of the clause piece by piece.

> And bind your feet / with the equipment of / the gospel of peace

The rendering of this verse in the box above is my own translation from Greek into English. You may be seeing many differences between my translation and that of your Bible. Basically, all you need to know is that I attempted to do an essentially "word for word" translation. It is not my goal to add any contextual notes within my translation here. Okay, back to the task at hand.

To "bind one's feet" would be best rendered in our modern day as "tie your shoes." The action is both active and reflexive. You must be the one to do the action to yourself. To "bind" implies what is being put on cannot be easily taken off. This will ensure what is put on will serve its intended purpose to the fullest of its ability. The natural question to ask next is, "With what should I bind my feet?" Paul says we bind our feet "with the equipment of..." The term I translated "equipment" is most commonly translated "preparation" or "readiness" in most Bibles. Paul is not describing a shoe like a tennis sneaker or a boot. Paul is describing a Roman sandal. This type of sandal had several straps that were tied around the wearer's calf muscle (see below).

Roman Military Sandals

When Paul discusses the *shoe*, he is discussing the straps that keep the sandal in place. The straps serve as the *equipment* that holds everything together.

Lastly, Paul finally gets around to the central point of the construct. The *equipment* (or the laces/straps) are the gospel of peace. In other words, the gospel of peace is what keeps the Christian firmly rooted where he needs to be. The idea of being "firmly rooted" is a profound theme throughout the Bible. Perhaps most notable is what the psalmist says is Psalm 1:3, "He is like a tree planted by streams of water that yields its fruit in its season, and its leaf does not wither. In all that he does, he prospers." A tree planted by streams of water will grow deep, strong roots that are constantly receiving proper nourishment. That tree will grow strong. It shall not be moved.

The gospel of peace is what holds the Christian in place. Everything we do must be rooted in the gospel. It is somewhat ironic that Paul uses the phrase "gospel of *peace*" when describing the Christian's armor. However, peace is something promised to the Christian. Even in the midst of spiritual warfare, the believer can have peace! What an amazing promise!

No Roman soldier would ever go into battle without his shield. In the same way, no Christian should ever go into the world without his faith. This is why Paul calls us to take up the "shield of faith." The shield that Paul refers to here would be approximately four feet long and two and one-half feet wide. It was held on the left arm to protect the body from spear and sword injuries. The shield was designed to protect the entire body, not just one specific part. As you saw earlier, when the shields are joined together, the entire group is protected from all sides. Faith operates in the same way. Faith is vital for the individual, but it is an absolute necessity for the entire group.

Faith in Greek is the word *pistis*, which can mean faith, belief, loyalty, trust, trustworthiness, or value. It is common for Greek to use one word where English may use many different words. It is also true that Greek may have many words for just one English word. Rather than separate the definitions, it is best here to view them together. Our shield is a shield of loyalty, belief, trust, and value.

The purpose of the shield according to Paul is to "extinguish the fiery darts of the devil." That doesn't seem right. Doesn't a shield protect against swords and spears? Does Paul call them "fiery darts" because Satan is in Hell (i.e., the lake of fire)? Again, it all makes sense when we look again at the Roman soldier.

First-century warfare thrived on fear tactics. Fear tactics describe what happens when one army attacks another army using methods intended to scare the opponent rather than to do physical harm. One of the most popular fear tactics in Paul's day was to use fire in a variety of ways. Perhaps the most famous form of fire fear tactics was to ignite the end of an arrow with fire and shoot it at oncoming opponents (see below).

Flaming Arrows

In some cases, the Roman soldier would place a wet piece of leather over his shield. This was to extinguish the flame of a fiery arrow if one were to become lodged into the shield. Though I do not believe Paul was intending to make this point, I think it should be made nonetheless. In order to extinguish the "fiery darts of the devil," there must be water involved. It is not enough to just have faith. One needs *obedient* faith.

The helmet of salvation is next. The helmet was not only used to protect the soldier's head but was used to mark the soldier as a Roman. Relatively few eastern peoples wore helmets into battle. However, western cultures utilized the helmet to protect the head and to serve as a marker of who was a soldier for a particular city or country. When one saw a Roman helmet, one knew exactly for whom that soldier was fighting.

Roman Helmet

Salvation serves as our helmet. Salvation is what marks the believer as belonging to God. Salvation is what allows us to hold our head up high in the midst of a dangerous world. We discussed the need for salvation, what salvation is, and how one can receive salvation in chapter 1. Because of this, I will not discuss salvation as a whole here. However, I encourage you to review that material and ask how it applies to the whole armor of God.

The last piece of the whole armor of God is not armor at all. Yet without the sword of the spirit, there would be no point in going to battle in the first place. The Christian does not have any other option other than going into battle because, as Paul said earlier, we are at war. The sword is a weapon intended to be used for close hand-to-hand combat. Here, Paul says the sword is "of the Spirit" and it is "the word of God." Let's look at these two phrases further.

Most people think that we know very little about the Holy Spirit. They say things like, "The Bible doesn't have much to say about him," or, "How can we know anything if he is so mysterious?" These are ignorant things to say. The Bible actually has a great deal to say about the Holy Spirit. One simply must open his eyes and look. To understand the sword of the Spirit in Ephesians 6:17, it is best to evaluate the construct in an equation-like format.

$$\text{The sword of the Spirit} = \text{the word of God}$$

When we think of the word of God, we likely think of our Bibles. There is nothing wrong with that. Our Bibles are truly the word of God. However, Paul's audience would have taken this passage to mean something different—not because we are wrong but because they did not have the Bible like we have it today. The Bible was still being written when the Ephesians would have read this letter. So, what is the word of God? This question could be answered in three ways: (1) the spoken word of God, (2) the incarnate word of God, and (3) the written word of God.

The spoken word of God is the reason we exist in the first place. The creation account of Genesis 1 states that God spoke all of creation into existence. That is a powerful word. When God said, "Let there be light," there was no other option for the light except that it come into being. In the same way, God's spoken word came to the patriarchs and the prophets. In many instances, the prophets received their messages to the people or to the king because "the word of YHWH (i.e., God) came upon" them. The spoken word of God is ultimate truth and power.

The phrase "the incarnate word of God" may seem a little bit technical. You know this better as Jesus Christ, God in the flesh. Look at how Jesus is depicted in John 1:1–5.

In the beginning was the Word, and the Word was with God, and the Word was God. He was in the beginning with God. All things were made through him, and without him was not anything made that was made. In him was life, and the life was the light of men. The light shines in the darkness, and the darkness has not overcome it.

John 1:14 then takes Jesus as a divine being who keeps his divinity but ultimately is found to be in the form and likeness of a man. Verses 1–5 call Jesus the "word" of God. Why? For the Jews, many understood the godhead of the Old Testament not as the Father, Son, and Spirit but as the Yahweh (YHWH; God), the Spirit of God, and Wisdom. In Greek, the term wisdom is the *logos*, which is translated "word." Therefore, the incarnate word (God in the flesh) is true wisdom.

The written word of God is what we have now. The people of the Old Testament had the spoken word by God himself and by the prophets. The people of Jesus day had the incarnate word, which is Jesus himself. Today, we have the written word—the Bible. The Bible is just as authoritative as the spoken and incarnate word. Remember, the Bible is not just one book. It is a collection of sixty-six different books that are all connected with one unifying theme—that is, salvation for those obedient to the will of God. The written word holds the same characteristics as the spoken and incarnate word. Each of these are *theopneustos*. This the Greek word often translated "inspired" in 2 Timothy 3:16. However, this word has a much more basic definition. *Theopneustos* is a Greek compound term. *Theos* means "God." *Theology* for example is the study of God. *Pneustos* means "breath," "wind," or "spirit." So, *theopneustos* literally means "God-breathed."

Roman Dagger

The sword of the Spirit is the word of God. A Roman soldier did not go into battle with the expectation that he would be using the sword for the majority of the fight. The Roman sword was a dagger-like knife. It was used in close hand-to-hand combat. I think understanding this is necessary to our application of this text. The word of God is not an ax or saber to be slung around in hopes of killing someone. It is a tool. Anyone can take up a long, double edged sword and go fight. Only a trained soldier can appropriately use a Roman sword (i.e., a dagger). When I began preaching, I would say in my sermons that the sword of the Spirit is not a weapon for mass destruction but a scalpel for heart surgery.

The Christian and Modesty

In 2018, I preached a sermon simply entitled "Modesty." To my knowledge, that topic had not been discussed at this congregation in many years. Some had told me that the last time someone tried to preach on the topic, it didn't end so well. People in American culture (or western culture for that matter) do not like to be told what they can and cannot do. Moral relativism and postmodernism have developed an ideology of individualism. Clothing is a form of expression. Therefore, we believe no one can tell us what we can and cannot wear. We believe that is an infringement on our right to express ourselves however we so desire. In addition, modesty is often addressed as a topic that only concerns females. We preach against low-cut shirts and short dresses. However, when Paul discusses modesty, he addresses both men and women. In the next few pages, I want to share with you some of my notes from that sermon. Wearing the armor of God or being clothed in Christ is necessary if we desire to follow Jesus. However, so is how we present ourselves physically. Let's explore why and how.

Modesty extends far beyond clothing for both men and women. Modesty is the presentation of a moderate, limited, and decent lifestyle. In other words, modesty NEVER revolves ONLY around clothing. Clothing is only a small part of modesty. Modesty then extends to how we live in every aspect of our lives. There is nothing wrong with having money, but living above your means or living selfishly is not living modestly. Take Philemon for example. He was a wealthy Christian in Colossae. Philemon 2 states that the Colossian congregation even met in his home. Philemon was able to utilize his wealth to aid the people of God (see also Lydia and Phoebe). Therefore, though he was wealthy, Philemon was able to live modestly.

When one thinks of the fall of man in Gen 3:1–7, one normally thinks of when Adam and Eve ate the forbidden fruit. This is certainly true. However, there are four sins presented within the whole narrative of the fall.

1. Eating the fruit of the tree of knowledge of good and evil
2. Eve being a stumbling block to Adam

3. Adam blaming Eve and Eve blaming the serpent
4. Improper covering of the body (i.e., immodesty)

When Adam and Eve sin, their eyes are opened so that they realize their nakedness. Nakedness meant nothing to them prior to this instance. However, once they discovered their nakedness, they immediately sought to cover themselves. Since they immediately sought to cover themselves, we can assume they understood nakedness to be something they perceived as bad. The Hebrew text implies they made "loincloths" for themselves from fig leaves. In other words, their clothing was only enough to cover their private areas (i.e., their genitals). As such, Eve would not have made a covering for her breasts—only her genitals. When God finds them, he sees that they have tried to cover themselves, but the way they had done it was still unsatisfactory to God. So, God made for them full body coverings from animal skins. This is the first time we see animals being killed in Scripture. This is because God requires the shedding of blood in order to cover sins (cf. Heb 10:1–10). The garments God fashioned for Adam and Eve were full-length garments. They went from the neck to the ankles. Their initial covering was insufficient. God's covering was complete.

Paul addresses both male and female modesty in 1 Tim 2:8–10.

> I desire then that in every place the men should pray, lifting holy hands without anger or quarreling; likewise, also that women should adorn themselves in respectable apparel, with modesty and self-control, not with braided hair and gold or pearls or costly attire, but with what is proper for women who profess godliness—with good works.

Paul begins with men in v. 8. We rarely think of men dressing immodestly, though many men do. However, think of how a man uses his money. Men are notorious for buying new vehicles, having the newest phone, or having the nicest clothes. When a man is immodest, it is usually a result of him flaunting his possessions. In order to properly understand what Paul is saying to both men and women, one must first understand a man's *mega-need* and a woman's *mega-need*. A "mega-need" is the overarching emotional need of a man and woman. Countless studies have been performed to determine what these emotional needs are. While the order and extent of the other needs can be varied, the mega-needs for men and women remain the same. So, let's begin with the man's mega-need—respect and honor.

Ladies, the only way you will ever properly communicate with your husband, son, father, etc. is to show him proper respect and honor. This does not mean that you must worship or glorify him to an elevated point. Paul makes this point in Ephesians 5:22 when he writes, "Wives, submit to your own husbands as to the Lord." Submission does not mean being "beaten down" or "degraded." It simply means to treat your husband with the same level of respect as you would treat Jesus.

This is important to understand because a man who needs respect and honor will get it any way that he can. It is oxygen in his world. We need oxygen to live but not every source of oxygen is a good source. Take for example carbon monoxide (CO_1). Carbon monoxide is very deadly even though it has one oxygen molecule. We need oxygen to live, but if we breath in carbon monoxide, we will die. It is poison. So too are the needs of men and women. Having the need is not a bad thing. Where and how one receives the fulfilment of the need is the challenge.

How is a man to practice a modest lifestyle? Paul gives four suggestions here in v. 8. Paul says, "I desire then that in every place the men should pray, lifting holy hands without anger or quarrelling." First, a man should be a godly example wherever he goes. Notice Paul's words "in every place." Not just at home or school or church but everywhere. Second, men need to learn to give God their issues. This is not to lessen the importance of a counsellor or therapist if one needs such help, but it is to say that Paul wants men to **pray**. Prayer is something most men do in public but rarely do in private. It is not a weak thing for a man to pray. Let God know exactly what you are feeling whenever you are feeling it. David did. Jesus did. Paul did. We should.

The third suggestion may be a little difficult to understand at first. What does Paul mean when he says, "lifting holy hands," and how does that apply to male modesty? The Jews did not pray in the same way that we do today. There was no "bow your head and close your eyes" in the 1st century or ancient Judaism. Instead, the men would stand lifting their hands and head to heaven and pray. While hand-raising may be viewed negatively by some, it was the way Paul would have prayed. (It is important to note that hand-raising is not found in the New Testament except as it is connected to the posture of prayer.)

Jewish Man Praying

I call this having "proper religious posture." Men, especially those who lead in the public assemblies of the church, have opportunities on a regular basis to show out. When Paul calls the men to pray lifting holy hands, he is calling the men to present themselves as reaching out for God. In the same way, we might say today that men should be humble, loving, gentle, and an example of one who is walking in the light.

Lastly, Paul says that men should replace wrath with love. Men should pray without anger or quarrelling. It is very easy as a man to be one who argues or engages in fierce debate. We men are the worst at thinking we know everything. On the other hand, it is very difficult for men to express love. Men are taught to be hardened to emotion. This is a terrible tragedy in our culture. Every component of the fruit of the Spirit has an enemy. The enemy of love is wrath. I cannot love someone if I feel wrathful towards them. Being a man of modesty means being a man who is not afraid to love.

Verse 9 switches the attention to women. While Paul does have words to say about clothing, that is not all he has to say regarding the issue. Just as we discussed the man's mega-need, so too must we discuss the mega-need for a woman. A woman's mega-need is for love and acceptance. If a woman cannot get her mega-need, she will seek ways to get it any way that she can. It is oxygen in her world. This is why God tells husbands in Ephesians 5:25 to "love your wives as Christ loved the church and gave himself for her." Unfortunately, the world is telling women that in order for them to be loved, they must have something to offer. As a result, many women feel like the only way they can receive love and acceptance is through their physical attributes. Ladies, if you believe this, please don't. Find a man who loves you for your inner person. Beauty fades. A godly character lasts a lifetime.

So, what should a godly woman wear? While much has been said on immodest clothing by many others, I submit a woman should wear *proper* clothing, not necessarily *prudish* clothing. Women can look beautiful in modest clothing. Trust me, I see it every day with my wife. Dressing modestly does not mean dressing in a burlap sack that goes down to your ankles. A general rule of thumb would be this: if I can't wear this to church, a youth group event, or around my own father, I don't need to wear it at all.

Paul speaks out against braided hair, pearls, and costly attire in v. 9. Yet, we see godly women in congregations today who are doing the exact opposite. Are they sinning? The short answer is, no. Paul was dealing with an issue that was prevalent in the churches of the Lycus River valley where Timothy was working. Apparently, the women of these churches had been bringing a great deal of attention to themselves by the way they dressed. The congregation was becoming more of a social club than the people of God (a common problem in today's congregations). It seems that Paul is not against any of these things as long as they are given their proper place. Many women in the 1st century possessed slaves whose sole purpose was to be their hairdressers. Most women wore their hair braided with pearls and gold or other precious metals woven into their hair. Not so different from today's world, a woman's looks were everything to her in the 1st century. However, clothing should be a picture frame for the face and inner person, not a silhouette of the body.

So, what should a woman wear? Fortunately, the only physical aspect of clothing on which Paul remarks is that it should be respectable. The other items are matters of the heart—self-control, godliness, and good works. There are several physically attractive women in this world who are incredibly ugly because of their inner person. Strive to have an attractive attitude. 1 Peter 3:1–2 speaks of women who can win their unbelieving husbands without a word. Again, this is not suggesting that a woman needs to be a quiet, beaten down shell of a person. Instead, being a gentle and quiet person is simply the opposite of being a rough and loud person. Believe me, I know several boisterous women. Being a godly woman means being *gentle*. Remember, God's presence was not in the storm but in the low whisper (1 Kgs 19:12).

What's the point of all this? Is this just another shot for the conservative preacher to come down on young people? No, not at all. The point is for us to understand that God's plan is 100% perfect. If God's plan is perfect, then we all have a 100% chance of success within it. God never sets a plan in motion with failure in mind. I am a preacher and a teacher. Honestly, I would preach sin and evil if it worked, but it doesn't. God's plan always works.

Most of the time, the discussion of modesty hinges on political correctness and careful speech. I hope, as we have discussed this topic, none of you have felt attacked or singled out. That is not the goal of this section. The goal is to establish men and women as total equals in significance but not in function. Men are given different jobs within Scripture that they must carry out (e.g., Elders, Deacons, ministers, fathers, sons). Likewise, women are given roles in Scripture that men can never fulfill (e.g., teaching younger women, serving in the home, raising children, mothers, daughters). Different functions do not belittle or elevate anyone under or over the other. They are assigned to us by God so that we may work within our given functions to the best of our ability. We are designed to fit together like puzzle pieces in the grand scheme laid out by God.

Getting Dressed

When I do premarital counselling, I stress communication as the key to a successful and happy marriage. According to a plethora of academic studies, approximately 93% of all communication is nonverbal. This means we communicate with each other by means of speaking words only 7% of the time. Even now I am communicating to you via nonverbal means. How one presents oneself is a form of nonverbal communication. This involves (but is not limited to) how we dress. When people look at us, are they seeing Christ or are they seeing Satan? How we dress and how we present ourselves will impact how we are received by other people. I cannot go door-knocking in my community and expect to see results if I am wearing a T-shirt with drug references on it. People will see me as hypocritical. Our message may be the message of God, but what I present nonverbally may not match his message. We need to be extremely careful about this.

God wants us to live in a way that reflects him. That is the whole point of this chapter. Living in Jesus Christ is not about us. It is about him. We are to be the mirror of Jesus. When people see us, they need to see the love, grace, mercy, and hope that is found in Christ. Growing up, I was told, "You may be the only Bible someone ever reads." That is a scary thought. Am I making it my life's goal to bring others to the Lord and serve him wholeheartedly, or am I placing all of my hope and desires in the world? As we end this section, remember the words of John when he writes, "Do not love the world nor the things in the world. If anyone loves the world, the love of the Father is not in him" (1 John 2:15). Let's wear the brand of "Christian" every day.

Personal Reflection

1. Is there any part of the **whole** armor of God that you are neglecting?
2. What is your morning routine? How can you fit God into that time?
3. Can others see Jesus when they see you? Why or why not?
4. What are some "accessories" that you are going to include in your spiritual wardrobe?
5. Do you need to throw out some of your clothes because they are immodest? How do you really want people to see you?

The Trail We Blaze

"For we **walk** by faith, not by sight."
2 Corinthians 5:7

"But I say, **walk** by the Spirit, and you will not gratify the desires
of the flesh."
Galatians 5:16

"And **walk** in love, as Christ loved us and gave himself up for us, a
fragrant offering and sacrifice to God."
Ephesians 5:2

"So as to **walk** in a manner worthy of the Lord, fully pleasing to him,
bearing fruit in every good work and increasing in the knowledge of
God"
Colossians 1:10

My wife and I love being outside. There have been many times where
we have found ourselves sitting at home glaring aimlessly at the TV
when one of us will say, "Hey, let's go for a walk." It's not that we
necessarily need the exercise (though I suppose I could benefit from
it). It's just that we love going from one place to another, seeing the
sights that lie along the way, and ultimately reaching our intended
destination.

In November of 2019, my wife and I celebrated our first
wedding anniversary. I, being the realist that I am, knew that we
would only get one *first* wedding anniversary. I felt strongly that we
needed to do something special before we had kids, pets, or other
responsibilities that would eventually come along with our marriage.

We both agreed that we may never get to take an anniversary trip with just the two of us ever again. We decided to go back to Ashville, NC. This is where we spent the very first day of our honeymoon. There, we would spend a day touring the Biltmore home. Later, we would spend another day hiking in the beautiful mountains of North Carolina. We had toured the Biltmore home once before while on our honeymoon; yet, we both felt rushed and, honestly, it was kind of an awkward feeling to be a newly married couple. So, we decided to do the tour again on this trip. Maybe we would actually pay attention this time.

The Biltmore home is the largest residential home in America. Its construction, completed in 1895, served as an engineering marvel for its day. The home had indoor running water, an indoor pool that would be filled and drained with each use, a bowling alley (I'm told this was the first bowling alley in America, but I'm not sure), a grand dining hall (among many other breakfast halls and other smaller dining areas), and many other things too numerous to name. We knew from our previous tour a year prior that it was going to take us a long time to tour this place again. In addition to touring the home, we had also bought tickets to tour the Biltmore winery. Regardless of your views on alcohol, one must admit the science and history behind wine making is fascinating. That's why we took the tour, in case you were wondering. Plus, we hoped to see the beautiful Biltmore vineyards. Unfortunately, we were only allowed to see the distillery. All in all, we spent the entire day on the Biltmore property. We did a lot of walking—more than I care to admit. I realized quite quickly that I am in no shape to walk that much in one day in shoes that are not built for walking long distances.

The second day was an incredibly beautiful day. The sun was shining, the temperature was perfect (if not a little chilly). The trail that was before us lay ready to be discovered. Don't forget, we had spent the entire previous day on our feet walking from one tour stop to the next. As you can imagine, we were both a little tired. I wasn't too worried, though, because this hiking trail was supposedly rated for beginners. We both agreed that the hike would not be too challenging.

The scenery was absolutely breathtaking. The trees were at the end of their full-color season, the birds and squirrels were running all over the place while a light breeze filled our lungs with the purest, fresh mountain air. That beauty, however, lasted for a total of five minutes. We should have known that climbing a trial on a mountain meant we would be walking up hill. For some reason (likely because the trail was rated for beginners) we did not really think about it. About half-way up the trail, I told my wife that I needed to stop and rest for a minute. Embarrassed, I admitted my calf muscles were beginning to cramp. I had not hydrated like I should have (having drank only one cup of strong black coffee that morning) and my muscles were still sore from the day before. I was unable to walk a simple beginner's trail because I began my journey unprepared.

I rested for about five minutes then began the climb again. The stream below the ledge on which we stood was rushing down the mountain while I was struggling to trudge the opposite direction. I was determined to reach the end of the trail. This particular trail ended with a beautiful waterfall (one of the highest falls in North Carolina). We both desperately wanted to see that waterfall in its true, natural beauty—not just in a picture. After what seemed like forever, we finally reached the viewing point for the falls. They were absolutely breathtaking. I wish I could describe the beauty here, but words would not do them justice. The cameras on our cellphones were unable to capture the true height of the falls. Words simply cannot describe nor can pictures show what we saw. We saw true beauty at the end of that trail.

Once you rise from the waters of baptism, you begin walking on your spiritual trail. Your journey begins right when you take the first step out of the baptistry. The problem comes, not when you first begin your walk (though that is certainly a possibility) but when you've been active in your walk for a little while. That's when you start to get tired and sore. While this book is mainly focused on how one might *begin* his or her faithful walk with Jesus, I do not want to neglect the ongoing journey in which we are all a part. That is the purpose of this chapter.

Highway to Hell or Stairway to Heaven?

Someone once said, "There's a reason there is a highway to Hell and a stairway to Heaven." I do not know who came up with this saying, but they are right. Getting to Heaven seems so difficult. Yet, going to Hell seems so easy. Notice the lyrics of AC/DC's famous song "Highway to Hell."

> Living easy, living free
> Season ticket on a one-way ride
> Asking nothing, leave me be
> Taking everything in my stride
> Don't need reason, don't need rhyme
> Ain't nothing I would rather do
> Going down, party time
> My friends are gonna be there too

The song suggests the way to Hell is a road of good times, parties, having fun, and just being human. Isn't that what we are though? We're only human right? Unfortunately, this is the approach most people take when it comes to their walk with God. We think, "It's okay if I mess up. I'm only human. I mean what does God really expect from me? He knows I'm not perfect, so why should I try to be?" (Note Rom 6:1–2)

For now, let's explore what it means to be human. Is being human a good excuse for sin? Didn't humans fail in the garden in Genesis 3? Yes. Yes, they did. However, being "only human" is never a good excuse to commit sin. In fact, no excuse is a good excuse for sin. We see that God's creation of humans is vastly different from any other created thing. Not only does God create humans from preexisting material (Gen 2:7), but God breathed life into humanity. This "breath of life" is the Hebrew word *nephesh*. This word can be translated as "life," "breath," "wind," "spirit," or "soul" depending on its context. Here, it means that God breathed *life* into humanity implying God as the giver of life. So, humans have life. I think since you're reading this, you already know you're alive. What a blessing! But it isn't enough for humans to just *be alive*. Animals are alive. But humans and animals are different. Humans are made in the image of God. But what does this mean? Honestly, there are a million different interpretations of this phrase. Probably over half of the million interpretations contain some amount of truth. I cannot discuss the fullness of the meaning honestly because I do not know the fullness of the meaning. I can only tell you what I know.

At its root, here's what being made in the image of God means, so far as I understand it. First, it means we have the ability to make right and wrong decisions. In other words, humans have a moral compass. No other creature on Earth has such a thing. Though God does not make wrong choices, God is certainly a moral being. God knows what is right and what is wrong. Second, it means that there is some part of us that reflects God. This may be the existence of a soul/spiritual nature, or it could refer to the ability to make decisions. Whatever it means, it is clear that humans are special to God.

Humans are the ones that Jesus came to save. Yes, John 3:16 says, "For God so loved the *world*," but what is the *world*? The *world* is a term used to describe all of creation. Ever since "the fall" in Genesis 3, the entire world has been impacted by sin (remember the earth sprouted thorns and thistles). Therefore, in Christ, the *world* is fully restored. Ultimately, this world of evil and decay will come to an end (2 Pet 3:10) and a new existence will be the reality. How this will happen will not be discussed here (let the reader understand). When Jesus died on the cross, he made a way of salvation for all of humanity—only humanity. That's you and me. So, saying that we are "only human" is nothing more than a terrible excuse for sin. Only humans are the ones who have salvation in Jesus Christ.

Why does it seem so easy to go to Hell and so difficult to go to Heaven? The latter part of this question will be explored in the following section. For now, let's focus on the first part. Unfortunately, no one likes talking about Hell. It is a very depressing topic. Most western Christians (i.e., American and European Christians) either do not believe in Hell or do not believe they are in danger of going to Hell. In fact, according to a study of the Pew Research Center conducted in 2015, 72% of Americans believe in Heaven, but only 58% believe in Hell.

There are a few misconceptions about Hell that we must explore. To begin, Hell is not a place for bad people. You've probably heard before that bad people go to Hell. Well, to an extent I suppose that is true because none are good except God alone (cf. Rom 3:10; Mark 10:18). All have sinned and fallen short of the glory of God (Rom 3:23). So, in reality, everyone is bad in comparison to God (see Chapter 1 for more on this subject). However, as we understand morally good and morally bad people, the fact is that there will be morally good people in Hell.

How can this be? Doesn't God want us to be morally good? Yes, he does. But therein lies the misconception. Hell is not a place for bad people. Hell is a place for those who reject God. Morally good people still reject God. You see, God is love (1 John 4:8). Because God is love, God cannot and will not force his creation to love him. This means God will not force us to be with him if we choose that we do not want to be with him. Hell is not a place for bad people. Hell is a place for unsaved people who have rejected God.

Hell is not something a Christian should fear. As a preacher, I hear on a regular basis that Christians are afraid of Hell. This notion prompted one of my best and most controversial sermons entitled, "Hell is a good thing and Heaven doesn't have it all." I know, long title, but go with me on this. The lesson was taken straight from Revelation 20–21. In this section of Scripture, God is revealing to the apostle John the eternal place of punishment for all evil things and the glory waiting for all holy things (i.e., those who are saved). In the sermon, I mentioned three reasons why Hell (to a Christian) should be interpreted as a good thing. First, Hell is Satan's final prison (Rev 20:10). Satan has already been defeated at the cross and will be completely rendered powerless when Jesus returns. To the Christian, this should be amazing news! No longer will Satan be able to attack us. The war against the evils of this world will then be over. We will one day not be at battle any more.

Next, Hell is Death's final prison. I capitalized "Death" here for a reason. In Revelation 20, Death is personified along with Hades. In other words, Hell will contain both *death* and the *realm of the dead.* "Hades" is the Greek term used to describe the afterlife and is also the name of the Greek god of the underworld. "Sheol" is the Hebrew term for the afterlife/underworld (i.e., the realm of the dead). In both Greek and Ancient Near Eastern mythology, the afterlife was a place where no one wanted to go. It was a bleak existence of souls wandering around hopelessly lost for eternity. However, God has informed us that Death (the original punishment for sin) and the realm of the dead (Hades/Sheol) will ultimately be contained in this prison called Hell. When the time comes, there will be no need for death and no need for a holding place of the dead. Why? Because the dead will be raised upon Christ's return (1 Thess 4:13–18). If the dead are raised, then there is no need for the dead to have a holding place. The dead will either be alive with Christ or enduring the second death.

What exactly happens when we die? The short answer is that we can only know what is told to us in Scripture. Not every aspect about every little thing has been revealed to us. Only what we need to know has been revealed. That being said, there are some things that can be known about this somewhat bleak topic. I think we are all aware that everyone—good or bad—will die unless the Lord returns during our lifetime. When we die, our bodies are lowered into the ground or perhaps our ashes are spread over a particular part of the world. Our souls, however, do not decay or cease to exist. Our souls are in a state of conscious existence (cf. Luke 16:19–31; Rev 6:9–11). Here, those who are righteous (in Christ) are given rest. Those who are not righteous (in Christ) are in a state of unrest (note the rich man in Luke 16 mentioned above). Eventually, the Lord will return to gather his people unto himself. The Bride of Christ (i.e., the church) will be united with the bridegroom (i.e., Jesus) at the marriage supper of the Lamb (Jesus is the Lamb of God). Those who are in Christ will be with Jesus, God, and the Holy Spirit for eternity where we will be his people and he will be our God. Those who are not in Christ will endure the second death (Rev 21:8). Below is a list of events as they are laid out in Scripture with their Scripture references given. I hope you will use this as a guide to explore the Scriptures to see what they say about the events yet to come.

- The Lord will descend from Heaven (1 Thess 4:16)
- The archangel will shout (1 Thess 4:16)
- The trumpet of God will be heard (1 Thess 4:16)
- The dead in Christ will rise (1 Thess 4:16)
- Those alive in Christ will be taken up (1 Thess 4:17)
- The Earth will be destroyed by fire (2 Pet 3:10)
- All people are judged (Eccl 12:13–14; Matt 12:36; Rev 20:11–15; Heb 9:27)
- New heavens and new earth are established as a place where righteousness dwells (2 Pet 3:13)
- The saved enter glory with God (Rev 21:3–4; 22:14; Matt 25:14–30)
- Those condemned are cast into Hell (Rev 21:8)
- Eternity ensues

Now, I admit, this is not the most fun topic to think about. However, it bears noting that we are all currently walking down a trail that will ultimately lead to one of these two realities. Either we are walking a path headed for Hell or on a path headed for Heaven. Though it may (as the AC/DC song suggests) be an easy thing to end up in Hell, it is not impossible for us or anyone else to make it to Heaven. Remember the words of Jesus in Matthew 7:13–14, "Enter by the narrow gate. For the gate is wide and the way is easy that leads to destruction, and those who enter it are many. For the gate is narrow and the way is hard that leads to life, and those who find it are few."

The Narrow Way

Unfortunately, as I was looking up various comments on Matthew 7:13–14 mentioned above, I was shocked to find very little said about it. Now, that does not mean others have not said more elsewhere. It simply means in my limited research, I did not find much. Perhaps more disturbingly, the sources that said the least about this passage were from commentaries written by members of the Lord's church. As is customary for writers in Christian circles, more is usually said concerning how to *become* saved as opposed to what one should do while one *is* saved. If you have been baptized into Christ, you are a saved person. Most preachers, teachers, and authors will go straight from the point of salvation to the return of Christ at the end of time (i.e., baptism to the eschaton). But not here. We are on a long and hard journey.

In Matthew 7:13–14, Jesus informs his audience that the way leading to life is a long and difficult road. Of course, in the 1st century most every road was a difficult one. Jesus audience would have known quite well about rough and treacherous roads. However, roads in this time period were not difficult because of their physical condition. Pot holes, road work, and repaving were not thoughts ancient people had about their roads. When Jesus mentioned a difficult road, his audience might have thought about those roads that were known to be violently dangerous. We can see a glimpse of this understanding in Jesus's parable of the good Samaritan. The man is travelling down the road when he "fell among robbers" (Luke 10:25–37). It was not uncommon for robbers to hide out alongside these roads and attack travelers. That would certainly make the way difficult. In the same way that robbers would hide alongside these roads in an attempt to harm and rob the traveler, Satan too is lurking along the narrow path. He will take any opportunity to attack us. He hates that we are going down the road less travelled. There is nothing Satan wants more than for you and me to be traveling down his road—the wide path. We must remember that Satan's road ultimately leads to nowhere (as Josh Turner's famous song *Long, Black Train* indicates). It is pretty easy to understand what Jesus is saying in Matthew 7:13–14. Each road is presented as the exact opposite of the other.

Satan's Way	Jesus's Way
Wide	Narrow
Many travelers	Few travelers
Leads to Destruction	Leads to Life

The way may be narrow, but it is as wide as it needs to be. This does not imply that God does not make a way for all to come to him. Rather, this means that, while the way is presented to all people, few will choose to accept the challenge.

For those of us who have accepted the challenge, how should we go on our journey? Paul says in Ephesians 4:1–3, "I therefore, a prisoner for the Lord, urge you to walk in a manner worthy of the calling to which you have been called, with all humility and gentleness, with patience, bearing with one another in love, eager to maintain the unity of the Spirit in the bond of peace." These verses provide the reader with instructions on how one should proceed down this narrow path.

Paul begins by making a plea for Christians to walk worthily of their calling. It is debated among various Christian circles whether or not individuals are "called" to come to God. I believe this to be a fruitless debate. Jesus makes it very clear in John 6:44 when he says, "No one can come to me unless the Father who sent me draws him. And I will raise him up on the last day."

This may seem like Jesus is being selective about those whom he wishes to be his people, but that could not be farther from the truth. The Father is working in the hearts of every man to draw each person to him. Unfortunately, most people reject the call of God. We, on the other hand, have accepted his calling. We must remember that the calling comes from God himself. Therefore, we are held to God's standard (more on this in the next chapter).

Next, Paul provides the reader with some descriptive terms that illustrate how one can live up to God's standard. They are listed below.

1. Humility
2. Gentleness
3. Patience
4. Bearing with one another
5. Love
6. Eager to maintain unity in the Spirit

Humility is best defined by what it is not rather than by what it is. To be humble is the opposite of being puffed up or proud. Literally, the word means "to bring low." When we humble ourselves, we are bringing ourselves low and counting someone or something else as greater in value than our own selves. This is exactly what Paul says in Philippians 2:3, "Do nothing from selfish ambition or conceit, but in humility count others more significant than yourselves." Paul goes on to explain in Philippians 2 that this is exactly what Jesus did when he came to Earth. Read slowly the words of Paul in Philippians 2:5–11.

Have this mind among yourselves, which is yours in Christ Jesus, who, though he was in the form of God, did not count equality with God a thing to be grasped, but emptied himself, by taking the form of a servant, being born in the likeness of men. And being found in human form, he humbled himself by becoming obedient to the point of death, even death on a cross. Therefore, God has highly exalted him and bestowed on him the name that is above every name, so that at the name of Jesus every knee should bow, in heaven and on earth and under the earth, and every tongue confess that Jesus Christ is Lord, to the glory of God the Father.

The humility of Jesus is mindboggling when one views him under Paul's microscope. Paul is able to explain Jesus's own words with the life of Jesus himself. Jesus said, "Whoever exalts himself will be humbled, and whoever humbles himself will be exalted" (Matt 23:12). This is exactly what Jesus did. The king of Heaven humbled himself to a death on the cross—a symbol of immense shame. As a result, God has now exalted him to a place of honor that is second to none.

Gentleness is a quality most Christians ignore. As a matter of fact, some of my atheist friends have told me that they refuse to believe in Jesus because of how his followers act. Christians can be cruel and harsh. I have no doubt you have experienced this in some way or another already. I only pray that you are not the one displaying this attitude, though many of us are guilty of such things. A gentle behavior does not imply that one must be a pushover or timid. "Gentle" is simply the opposite of "rough." We like to respond to negative situations with a negative attitude. We often yell and scream and throw our temper-tantrums. However, being a Christian does not mean that we cannot feel angry or upset. Remember, Paul says, "Be angry and sin not" (Eph 4:26). It simply means that we respond to negative situations with the love of God. People should not see Christians as a threat. They should see Christians as a welcomed part of their lives. This should ultimately allow them to see God as a welcomed part of their lives.

"Patience" might be the most difficult term for me to discuss in this entire chapter. The English word *patience* comes from the Latin word *patientia*, which literally means "to suffer." We think being patient just means waiting a little bit longer than expected for what we want. We might go to a restaurant and be told our table will not be ready for another thirty minutes. We huff and groan until someone says, "Don't worry. Just be *patient*." That's not exactly the idea that patience is conveying here. If there is not some form of suffering involved, you haven't really experienced true patience. Patience is what Jesus showed his disciples the night before he died. Patience is what God shows us now. Peter writes in 2 Peter 3:9 that the reason Christ has not yet returned is because God is patient toward us. In other words, God is waiting for all people to come to a knowledge of him.

Paul's next phrase, "bearing with one another in love" is interesting to say the least. The term *bearing* might better be rendered "lift up" or "esteem" one another in love. I think Paul saying that love is what holds the Christian community together. Love is the Christian's glue. It is how we esteem one another and encourage one another.

God is love. God so loved the world that he gave Jesus to die for our sins. God loves his creation. Jesus even said that his disciples will be known by their love (John 13:35). Unfortunately, many Christians want to prove their discipleship by the name that is on the building where they worship or by their biblical intelligence level. However, that is not what Jesus says. Jesus says we will be known by our love for each other. At the time of this writing, love is something that is pressed in the media but rarely exemplified in culture. The modern world screams, "Love everyone! Love everything!" Yet, when someone disagrees with someone else, that person is then accused of hatred. Paul warns us to "speak the truth in love" in Ephesians 4:15. It is only by this approach that the gospel will ever be spread in our world.

Lastly, Paul says Christians must be "eager to maintain the unity of the Spirit in the bond of peace." Christian unity might be Paul's biggest concern in all of his letters. In fact, the issue of unity, not only within local congregations but in religious circles (e.g., among the Jews and the Gentiles) was so big of an issue to Paul that I included an entire appendix on Paul's doctrine of unity in my commentary on Paul's letter to Philemon (2019). The entire book of Ephesians has a running theme of God bringing things together. In Ephesians 1:10, Paul introduces Christian theology by stating that God has brought Heaven and Earth together in Jesus. In the whole chapter of Ephesians 2, Paul discusses the coming together of the Jew and Gentile into one body (i.e., Jesus's body, the church). In Ephesians 5, Paul discusses the coming together of man and woman in marriage echoing Genesis 2:24–25. In the same way that Paul discusses marriage, Paul also discusses the church and Christ. The church is the bride of Christ. It is the ultimate purpose of the church to be literally united to Christ. This will not happen until Christ's return. The following paragraphs are taken from my commentary *Paul's Letter to Philemon: A Historical and Exegetical Commentary*, pp. 133–34:

It may seem at this point that Paul's picture of the church excludes individualism. Even today, the church is divided because people say things like, "I can express myself better in this way," or, "I like the way this works more than the other way." This certainly is not the picture of unity Paul had in mind. The imagery of a *body* serves well in the description of what the universal group of Christians are to be.

When Paul discusses being a part of the body of Christ, he often makes the point that a body is composed of different parts working together to create a whole working form. In other words, each part must come together with the others or else the body cannot exist. This is made clear in Rom 12:4–5, "For as in one body we have many members, and the members do not all have the same function, so we, though many, are one body in Christ, and individually members one of another." Paul offers a type of commentary on this idea in 1 Cor 12:12–31 where he notes that once one has been baptized into Christ, one becomes a member of that body. Each member has a function. This implies rather forcefully that no member is useless or worthless. As a Christian, my life is hidden with Christ in God (Col 3:3), I am clothed in Christ (Gal 3:27), and I am a member of his body (Col 1:24). However, as part of this body, each individual has certain roles that allow the body to function at its fullest potential.

The unity of the body through individual parts also signifies that the body shares in feeling and emotion. In other words, when one part of the body is in pain, the whole body becomes aware. Imagine you are getting up at 2:00 in the morning for a glass of water. You stumble out of bed only to hit your littlest toe on the edge of the bed. You immediately inhale a deep breath. Your heart races. You reach down to grab your toe while your leg lifts your foot to your hand. Perhaps you jump up and down a few times. Maybe you exclaim, "Ouch!" Whatever the case may be, it is clear that the whole body is aware of the pain though the pain is only a problem for the littlest toe. The church must operate in the same way. Remember when the Lord appeared to Saul in Acts 9? Remember his first words to Saul? He said, "Saul, Saul why are you persecuting *me?*" (emphasis added). We do not know the names of those (besides Stephen) that Paul persecuted. We do not know their background, their lifestyle, or anything else about them. All we know is that they belonged to "the Way" (Acts 2:2). Yet, when these people suffered, the Lord knew it. He knew because he felt the pain of his body.

Let's not forget that this "unity" is of the Spirit and can only be found in the bond of peace. Peace is what holds unity together. However, every godly thing has its ungodly enemy. The enemy of peace is strife. Strife is what tears unity apart. It is important to note that *strife* and *disagreement* or *conflict* are not synonymous terms. In other words, unity can exist even when there is disagreement and conflict within the church. However, it is important to note that disagreement and conflict can eventually become strife if it is not resolved. This is why Jesus says, "So if you are offering your gift at the altar and there remember that your brother has something against you, leave your gift there before the altar and go. First be reconciled to your brother, and then come and offer your gift" (Matt 5:23–24). Note also Jesus's words in Matthew 18:15–17:

> If your brother sins against you, go and tell him his fault, between you and him alone. If he listens to you, you have gained your brother. But if he does not listen, take one or two others along with you, that every charge may be established by the evidence of two or three witnesses. If he refuses to listen to them, tell it to the church. And if he refuses to listen even to the church, let him be to you as a Gentile and a tax collector."

It doesn't take long for an argument to become a threat to unity. Peace, therefore, as a component of the fruit of the Spirit, is the only cure.

One Foot in Front of The Other

Each of the things mentioned above must be in the life of the Christian. This is how we are able to walk down the narrow path. No one said it would be easy. Certainly, there will be times when we trip and fall. Satan will put stumbling blocks along our way. They may come in the form of temptations, bad influences, broken relationships, or various other things. Just remember that Jesus is always there to pick us up and help us along the way. The trail we blaze is only travelled by placing one foot in front of the other.

When I first came to my own faith in Jesus, I couldn't help but wonder, "Why am I even doing this? I know I'm going to fail." For me, failure has never been an option. My wife tells me constantly that I am a perfectionist. I suppose that is true. After all, I take after both of my parents who are, for better or for worse, perfectionists. As a perfectionist, the last thing I want to do is fail my Lord. The problem is that I fail him on a regular basis. Perhaps you have found yourself doing the same thing.

Look, temptation is not fun. Being tempted implies that the thing you are facing is intrinsically wrong. If you have to debate whether you should or should not do something, you probably just shouldn't do it. Knowing you shouldn't do something and actually not doing it, however, are two different things. Is it wrong for us to desire a temptation? At what point does the temptation become sin?

Let's take the first question first. In short, it is not wrong to be tempted or to even desire a temptation. Just look at Jesus! In Matthew 4:1–11, Jesus goes to the wilderness so he can fast for forty days. Fasting is when someone does not eat food in an attempt to humble oneself before God. (For more on the topic, see *Should Christians Fast? A Study of Contemporary Spirituality from Matthew 6:1–18* by Joshua Houston.) This is usually a time of intense prayer and meditation. Jesus is using this opportunity to grow closer to the Father before he begins his earthly ministry. Being without food for forty days would surely cause severe hunger. At this time, Jesus was physically weak and desperately hungry.

The time when Jesus was his most vulnerable was when Satan showed up. Jesus is physically weak. He is incredibly hungry. So, Satan asks Jesus to turn a stone into a piece of bread. That would solve Jesus's problem, wouldn't it? Satan and Jesus both knew that Jesus had the power to do such a thing. There is nothing intrinsically wrong with eating bread, so why did Jesus refuse? What was the temptation? If Jesus had obeyed Satan, then Jesus would have submitted to Satan's will rather than to God's will. Therefore, Jesus refuses to turn the stone into bread. Instead, Jesus feeds on the word of God (Matt 4:4). This theme is carried out throughout the remainder of Jesus's temptations. This encounter with Satan in Matthew 4:1–11 is one reason that the writer of Hebrews could say:

> Since then we have a great high priest who has passed
> through the heavens, Jesus, the Son of God, let us hold
> fast our confession. For we do not have a high priest
> who is unable to sympathize with our weaknesses, but
> one who in every respect has been tempted as we are,
> yet without sin. Let us then with confidence draw near
> to the throne of grace, that we may receive mercy and
> find grace to help in time of need (Heb 4:14–16).

Jesus was tempted in every way that we are tempted today, though he never fell to those temptations. He never allowed his temptations to become sin. It's nice to have someone available who has encountered exactly what you are going through. We can always lean on Jesus.

Paul writes in 1 Corinthians 10:13, "No temptation has overtaken you that is not common to man. God is faithful, and he will not let you be tempted beyond your ability, but with the temptation he will also provide the way of escape, that you may be able to endure it." Every temptation has a "way of escape." In other words, when Satan tempts us, God has also provided a way out of that temptation. Let me give you an example. Let's say you have been watching pornography on your cellphone. You know doing this is wrong. You know it is going to hurt your spouse or your significant other. You know the people who are on that screen are real people with real souls. Yet, you can't seem to stop watching. Is there a way of escape? Yes, there is. Unfortunately, the way of escape in this particular scenario, along with many other scenarios, goes beyond simply saying "No." Addictions don't work like that.

Remember how we said that the church is a community of believers? As such, we are responsible for each other. In this particular scenario, I would recommend that the individual with the problem give his phone's password to a good friend or spouse. Then this person could set up the phone where these websites are blocked. In addition to blocking the temptation, the individual facing the temptation should be able to reach out to this person at any time of the day for emotional and spiritual support. This is true for all temptations. We need people who can and will hold us accountable for our actions.

The trail we blaze is a long and difficult road. But it is not impossible to walk it together with your Christian family and with Jesus. Though the trail may be difficult to travel, the end result will always be worth it.

Personal Reflection

1. What is currently keeping you from walking down the narrow path?
2. Do you have Christian friends who can hold you accountable? Will you let them hold you accountable?
3. Why does it seem so easy to sin and yet so difficult to be a person of righteousness?
4. How can you help someone else handle and control their temptations?

Progress, Not Perfection

"Like newborn infants, long for the pure spiritual milk, that by it you may grow up into salvation"
1 Peter 2:2

"But grow in the grace and knowledge of our Lord and Savior Jesus Christ. To him be the glory both now and to the day of eternity."
2 Peter 3:18

"And so, from the day we heard, we have not ceased to pray for you, asking that you may be filled with the knowledge of his will in all spiritual wisdom and understanding, so as to walk in a manner worthy of the Lord, fully pleasing to him, bearing fruit in every good work and increasing in the knowledge of God"
Col 1:9–10

Growth. That was all we wanted. They were so small. We couldn't make a profit if they were to stay the way they were. They were tiny, pink, annoyingly loud, and not exactly the best smelling things on the planet. We knew that we had to do something different. We tried feeding them regular food like we would anything else, but they weren't producing the desired output. We had to go a different route. I must admit, having a father who works as an animal nutritionist was a huge benefit to this situation. I take it you are probably lost as to what is going on here. Let me clarify.

As I mentioned earlier, I was blessed to grow up on a farm in Unionville, TN—the absolute middle of nowhere. My family raised sheep, cattle, goats, hogs, horses, and chickens among other things I'm sure. When I was in high school, my brother and I were very active in our local FFA and 4-H clubs. Let's just say I wasn't exactly the greatest athlete to walk the face of the Earth nor did I enjoy athletics to a great degree. My heart was (and always will be) on the farm. In 4-H and FFA, you must pick a "project" (i.e., an area of focus) in which to participate. Most students pick only one project. I, on the other hand, chose three: leadership, beef cattle, and swine. My brother and I took a great interest in showing shorthorn cattle and market hogs in our local and state FFA and 4-H shows.

We would buy our hogs when they were approximately 50-75 lbs. Trust me, that's tiny for a hog. We would then feed these hogs until they were of show quality (approx. 350 lbs.). That's a lot of growth in a short period of time (only a few months at the most). But, as mentioned earlier, having a father who is an animal nutritionist does have its advantages. My dad was able to formulate a specific diet for our hogs based on their nutritional needs. This way, the hogs would not only grow in size but also in quality. The *biggest* hog is not guaranteed to be the *best* hog. A fat hog may outweigh the rest but his muscle quality and the structural soundness of his bones will certainly be lacking. We did not want growth alone. We wanted quality growth. We wanted our hogs to make a grand transformation.

Never in a million years would I have thought that raising pigs would help me teach a lesson in progressing as a Christian. In complete honesty, there are actually a lot more lessons from these gentle giants that could be taught along with this one. For example, when you play with pigs, don't be surprised when you come out smelling like them. Or, don't get between two pigs fighting because they will eat you alive! But, I digress. Now that we have discussed why you decided to be a Christian and we've noted some tips on how to keep sin and temptation at bay, it is important that we discuss the growing process in Christ—not just existing in Christ.

The Challenge

What does it mean to be *perfect*? Think about that question. Ponder your answer. Got it? What did you think? Maybe you said something like:

"Being perfect means never making a mistake."

OR

"Being perfect means never committing a sin."

OR

"Being perfect means being whole and complete."

I'm sure you have other answers to this question than what is listed above. That's completely fine. All of these answers and perhaps your other answers as well have some element of truth to them. If someone is reciting a monologue in a word-for-word fashion, *perfection* would only be reached when the speaker finished speaking the words without making any mistakes. On the other hand, spiritual *perfection* is the absence of sin. We often say that Jesus was *perfect* because he had no sin (see 2 Cor 5:21 and 1 John 3:5). What about being *complete*? Imagine you have a pie, but a huge slice is missing. Is the pie complete? No. So, can the pie be truly *perfect* in its current state? Not if the definition of *perfection* requires the pie to be *complete*. *Perfection* is obviously a loaded word. We imagine the definition based on its context and our own presuppositional understanding. I want you to read the following verse very slowly and very carefully. This verse was not among those at the beginning of the chapter, so it should be fresh and new in your mind. Be sure to ponder it diligently. Okay, here it is:

> "Be perfect as your heavenly father is perfect" (Matt 5:48)

Tall order, don't you think? Could Jesus really be demanding our literal perfection? Doesn't he know that humans aren't perfect (as we have established all throughout this book). What could this verse possibly mean?

First, we must understand the verse in its literary context. In other words, we will gain an understanding of this verse based on the other verses that are around it. Remember, the Bible did not originally have chapter and verse divisions. Matthew 5 begins Jesus's great "sermon on the mount." In Matthew 5–7, Jesus took what was known through the law of Moses and transformed it in a way that shows what the law of God looks like when existing purely in God's kingdom. Jesus himself is the fulfillment of the law of Moses. He is the promised "kingdom bringer." The Jews of that day were actively looking for God's kingdom; yet, when it finally came, they did not recognize it. They were expecting an earthly kingdom with an earthly king. They were expecting the messiah to establish his throne in Jerusalem and destroy all other world powers, especially those annoying Romans. Of course, that is not what they received with Jesus. Jesus was the meek, humble, and lowly king. Jesus was the one who ate with sinners—something no real king would ever do. In the 1st century, eating with someone showed that you were friends with that person. Jesus was the friend of sinners. Jesus healed the sick even when others said he shouldn't. Jesus as the "kingdom bringer" was showing his audience exactly what living in the kingdom of God looked like.

So, what does it look like to live in the kingdom of God today? If an immigrant came to America, he would be required (at least legally) to undergo a series of tests on American history, government, culture, etc. In addition, while America does not have a true national language, the immigrant would do well to learn conversational English. He would have to learn how to use different units of measurements like miles, Fahrenheit, gallons, feet, and inches. In essence, the immigrant would be living in a different world.

When we are transferred into the kingdom of God, we find ourselves living in a whole new world. This is a world where Jesus is king, the Spirit guides our lives, and God himself is present with us. To understand this idea, we must first understand what it looks like to be in the presence of God.

Let's start at the very beginning. In Genesis 1–3, God was tangibly and literally with his creation. If we step back from the fall narrative of chapter 3 and the specifics of the creation narrative in chapter 1, we have a broader brush with which to paint this picture in chapter 2. There are two words that sum up the whole of Genesis 1–3. Those are "good" and "bad." When God created the world and things in the world, he called it "good." At the very end of the creation narrative in chapter 1, he looked at what he had made and called it all "*very* good." Thus, everything in the world is intrinsically good and only extrinsically made evil. Before Adam and Eve committed their sins, God was able to be with them in the garden in an unveiled state. In other words, there was nothing separating God from his creation. Thus, here is the first point about living in God's kingdom: God must exist in an unveiled state. In other words, God is not some distant theological idea. That is a Platonist deistic view of God—one that is not biblically accurate. The Greek philosopher, Plato, popularized the idea that "the gods" existed far away somewhere and had nothing to do with their creation. Therefore, as long as we don't make the gods mad, we'll be free to do as we please. Unfortunately, this line of thinking has permeated the theology of Christians today. We view God as being distant and uncaring. But this is not how the Bible depicts God. God is personal and active (Acts 17:22–31). Living in the kingdom of God means living with God. Notice what Paul says concerning this matter:

"In him we live and move and have our being" Acts 17:28

However, we cannot exist with God without undergoing some major adjustments—much the same as a new immigrant learning a new culture. For Adam and Eve to exist unveiled with God, they had to be part of the "perfect" creation. When they became "imperfect" or "sinful," that relationship was broken, though God was still around. He was and still is active in the world. The only difference is that there is now a veil between humanity and God.

I think we learn a lot from the tabernacle narrative in Exodus concerning how we can get close to God though sin still exists. The tabernacle/temple served as the one place on Earth where man and God could come together—much the same as the intended purpose for the garden in Genesis 2 and the church in 1 Corinthians 3:16. However, one could not just freely walk into the temple without first having some prerequisites. For starters, only the priests could serve in the temple. Further, only the High Priest could go into the Holy of Holies (that's where the ark of the covenant was) on only one day of the year known as *Yom Kippur* or the Day of Atonement. But wait! He could not enter the place where God truly was until he had been ceremonially washed, clothed in his priestly garments, ritualistically purified himself, and was deemed clean to enter. That may sound insane to us, but if we are in Christ, we too have done that very thing. Peter says that we are a royal priesthood (1 Pet 2:9). We have been clothed in Christ (Gal 3:27). We have been washed by the blood of Jesus (Acts 22:16). Therefore, we can approach the holy place in confidence (Heb 10:19).

You may be thinking, "Okay, yeah, but the temple doesn't exist today so how can we come in contact with God? Isn't he just off in Heaven somewhere?" This is a tragic understanding most Christians have today. God is personally with his creation in Genesis 2–3. That has always been God's intention and will be the final result upon Christ's return (Rev 21:3).

Paul's words in 1 Corinthians 3:16 and 6:19–20 are often either ignored or misunderstood. Paul writes, "Do you not know that you are God's temple and that God's Spirit dwells in you?" and "Or do you not know that your body is a temple of the Holy Spirit within you, whom you have from God? You are not your own, for you were bought with a price. So, glorify God in your body." In these passages, the term "you" is found in the plural form referring to the church (i.e., the Christians as a collective group). The Spirit also works individually by serving as the Christian's assurance of salvation (Eph

1:3–14). While some take this to be an allowance for miraculous powers, others interpret the passage to mean that the Spirit actually does not dwell within the heart of the Christian, but through the Scriptures only. It is beyond the scope of this book to evaluate these views in depth. However, I think the truth of these passages are not to be missed. Both passages state clearly that Christians as the body of Christ are the new temple. We have been made holy in Christ; therefore, we are now suitable places for God to exist. We are in him and he is in us. Being perfect as our heavenly father is perfect is impossible to do by ourselves. Fortunately, we are made perfect in Jesus Christ. His blood makes us clean before God. Being perfect does not mean that we will never make a mistake or commit a sin. It simply means that we are to be complete, clean, and holy in Christ.

The Truth

No one is perfect. I think you already knew that. It doesn't take long for one to look at our world and see its imperfection—not least to look at ourselves and see the same thing. We often think, "Well, at least I'm better than that person. I mean come on! I would never cheat on my spouse or abuse my children. I can't be that bad." I certainly would hope not. However, more often than not, these "bad things" we become so judgmental over are not committed by the heathens of this world. These sinful acts are committed by Christians. Today, the divorce rate among Christians is the highest it has ever been. The acceptance of homosexuality among Christians is climbing each day. I do not mention these issues to suggest that one person is better or worse than anyone else. I only hope to illustrate this one fact: Christians are not immune to sin.

We have already evaluated 1 John 1:7 at some length in this short book. Perhaps what we have neglected to this point is a deeper study of 1 John as a whole. Though space will not allow for a full exegesis of the book, we can certainly understand its main message as it pertains to our growth process.

John is writing to Christians. This means he is writing to those who have done what I assume you also have done—become part of the body of Christ. Understanding this fact, John's first two chapters addresses the struggle between the people of God and the world in which we live. For John's original audience, issues such as persecution, idolatry, and false teaching in the church were all rampant. One of these false teachings was the doctrine of Gnosticism. That's a weird word. Gnosticism comes from the Greek word *gnosis* which means "knowledge." Gnosticism taught two primary doctrines to which we must turn our attention further. First, Gnosticism taught that in order to be *truly* saved, one must have a special revelation of knowledge given to him from God. It was as if there was a secret that was hidden away by God just waiting to be discovered. However, we know this cannot be true. Paul tells us that God has made known the mystery to all who are in Christ (Eph 1:9).

Second, and more importantly here, Gnosticism taught that all of fleshly things (the physical) is inherently evil and all of the soul or spiritual things (the metaphysical) is intrinsically good. Therefore, if one sins, it doesn't matter, because sin only impacts the flesh and not the soul. The soul was viewed by these Gnostics as some orb of energy that sought to be released from the evil of the fleshly body. Of course, this idea is not compatible with Scripture. Perhaps C. S. Lewis puts it best when he said, "We are not bodies that have a soul. We are a soul that has a body." Physical bodies were created by God and deemed good in Genesis 1 and 2 as we have previously discussed. Thus, Gnosticism's analysis of the body and soul as evil or good is sadly mistaken on many levels. (These levels are too expansive to cover here.)

So, now that we know the intended audience of John's letter (i.e., Christians) and the issues facing the intended audience (i.e., persecution and false teaching), we can better establish why John writes what he does in his letter. Actually, John tells us why he writes this letter in 1 John 2:1–2.

> My little children, I am writing these things to you so that you may not sin. But if anyone does sin, we have an advocate with the Father, Jesus Christ the righteous. He is the propitiation for our sins, and not for ours only but also for the sins of the whole world.

When I was in school at Freed-Hardeman University, I took a class called "James through Jude." In this class, we studied the letters of James, Jude, 1 and 2 Peter, and 1, 2, 3 John. When it came time to study 1 John, my teacher, Dr. Kirk Brothers, assigned what he called a "theme phrase" to the book. That phrase was simply, "Know that you know that you know." In other words, the whole point of John's letter is to show faithful Christians that they can be sure of their salvation. This is one of many reasons why I love John's letter. John doesn't sugar-coat the reality of being a Christian. John says that he is writing these things "so that you may not sin." Then he writes, "but *if* you sin…" implying the potential that the Christian could and would still sin. So, here's the truth. You will sin as a Christian, but your sin is not the end of the story. We have already discussed Jesus's willingness to help you along your spiritual journey. However, we have yet to discuss what it means for Jesus to serve as our advocate.

The word "advocate" is the Greek word *paraklēton* (where we get our word *paraclete* or "helper"). The same word is used to describe the role of the Holy Spirit to the apostles in John 14:16. The word basically means "one who helps" or "one who comforts." Literally, it is one who inserts oneself into a situation for the purpose of offering aid in times of trouble. Though this is not the best illustration, the role of Jesus here could be described like that of a lawyer.

Imagine you are on trial for a crime you actually did commit. You were caught red-handed. There is no doubt in anyone's mind that you actually committed the offence. There is video evidence of your crime. You aren't getting off with a warning. Your trial begins. You know you are going to receive a horrible sentence. You, of course, deserve such a sentence. There is nothing you can do to stop the inevitable.

However, the court has appointed a lawyer to serve on your behalf. This guy is the best lawyer in the business. Instead of pleading your case to the judge, the lawyer tells the judge that he will pay the penalty for your crime. The judge deems this acceptable. You are now free to go. We touched on this truth earlier in the book, but one thing we did not discuss was *how* Jesus inserted himself into our situation. That's what a *paraclete* does. A *paraclete* sees a hopeless situation and runs directly toward it. Jesus saw us when we were down and out. He put himself in our place. He is the atoning sacrifice for our sins. Yes, we will still sin as Christians because we still exist in a fallen world, but Jesus is always there to be our advocate as long as we repent and continue to live in true repentance.

The Process of Progress

Perfection is not achieved overnight. Further, we have established that being truly perfect in every single way is an impossibility for the human state. However, there are things we can do to **grow** in the grace and knowledge of our Lord Jesus Christ (2 Pet 3:18). Below are five simple suggestions. In order for these suggestions to bear results, you must be willing to incorporate them into your very essence of being. It will not be enough to do these things once a month or even once a day. These things must be as important to you as breathing, eating, or sleeping.

1. Don't just read the Bible. Study the Bible. At the time of this writing, I am teaching a Bible class on the book of Genesis. When I teach, I try my best to go verse by verse carefully looking at the wording of the verse while still retaining the overall theme of the book and the purpose of God as it is presented throughout his whole story of the Bible. Genesis is, of course, the best place to start. It was only coincidental that one night during my time teaching Genesis, I received a phone call from my brother. My brother went to Freed-Hardeman University for both undergraduate and graduate school. However, he pursued degrees in Business, not in biblical studies. My brother knows the Bible (and knows it well), but he does not have the formal training or exposure to certain ideas and theories like I do. At any rate, he called me one night because he had been casually reading through Genesis, making it without any trouble through the first seventeen chapters of the book. However, chapter 18 was not so simple.

For context, Genesis 18 is the chapter where the three "men" tell Abraham and Sarah that they will have a son one year from that conversation. Neither Abraham nor Sarah believe these messengers. They were both so old! However, one year later, Isaac is born. The question that my brother (and countless others) asked was this: who exactly are these three men?

The easy answer is that the text does not tell us. However, many interpretations have been presented nonetheless. Some believe the three men to be the Father, the Son, and the Holy Spirit. Others believe they are three angels who appear in the form of men. Still some believe they consist of God and other two angels (this is my personal view). Ultimately, the text does not tell us. What we are left with is the knowledge of divine revelation (i.e., a son will be born) and divine destruction (i.e., the destruction of Sodom and Gomorrah).

This story illustrates the great challenge of studying the Bible, not just reading it. There is a huge difference between *reading* and *studying*. Reading can be done half-heartedly. Studying, however, forces the reader to think about the text and the purpose behind the text. While several other books (much more robust than this one) have been written about Bible study and biblical interpretation (called hermeneutics), here are a few things to keep in mind that will help you get all you can from the text.

First, remember that the goal of the text is to ultimately tell the story of God. The text is not designed to harmonize with science or even reveal some hidden secret about mankind. The text is designed to tell the story of God and to reveal God to his beloved creation.

Second, remember the human author and his purpose for writing. For example, one reason the Gospel of John is so different from the other three Gospels is because John's purpose is different. John says that he wrote his Gospel so that "you might believe" (John 20:31). This is called *authorial intent*. Ask yourself, "Why did the author write what he did in the way that he did? What was his personal experience at the time of writing?"

Next, remember who the original audience is. Take Matthew and Luke's Gospels for example. Matthew wrote with the intention of his Gospel being read by the Jewish community. Matthew, a Jew himself, uses language and themes that would have been well known to the Jewish community of his day (e.g., using the term "kingdom of heaven" rather than "kingdom of God"). Luke, however, was a gentile writing to a gentilic audience (see Luke 1:3; Acts 1:1). This should impact how we read each Gospel. The letters of Paul are another good example. When Paul writes to Corinth, he is addressing specific problems in that particular congregation. When Paul writes to the Colossians, Paul is writing with the Colossian church in mind. Understanding the audience is crucial to understanding the meaning of the text.

There are many more things that could be noted here on this topic. Nevertheless, we must press on. As you study, try to notice various themes (e.g., God as savior, the call to repentance, etc.) and theological words (e.g., love, joy, grace, mercy, etc.). Underline or highlight these words and phrases in your Bible. Don't be afraid to make notes as you study. Study daily. It would be very beneficial for you to have your own study that is not reliant on what you are being taught at church. Study because you want to know God.

2. Rejoice always. Unfortunately, Christians have a bad habit of looking like they are eating dill pickles all day long. If you didn't catch the meaning of that image, it basically means that most Christians act miserable all the time. Christians are known for wearing a frown. Not only that, but we live in a world that glorifies the miserable. Have a mental health issue? Post about it on social media and get a swarm of fake attention rather than seek true, professional help. Do you feel tired even though you slept for ten hours last night? You must need a break from work or school.

Okay, I admit I am being a little harsh here. But you see my point. Being miserable is glorified in today's world. However, at a time when people actually had the right to be miserable due to dangerous food shortages, bad governmental leadership, and immense persecution, Paul commands the Christians in Philippi to "Rejoice in the Lord always. Again, I will say, Rejoice!" (Phil 4:4). The verb *rejoice*, as it exists in its original Greek form, is an imperative verb. That means (basically) that Paul is issuing the command for the Philippian Christians to rejoice!

It is possible to rejoice when we are not happy. Happiness is the result of an external influence. In other words, things outside of our own existence cause us to be happy like getting a new car or finding money in your pocket you didn't know that you had. Joy, on the other hand, comes from within ourselves. Joy is a gift of the Spirit. If you are in Christ, you have a reason to rejoice! So, rejoice!

3.   Pray without ceasing. Paul doesn't only issue the command to rejoice to the Philippians. He also gives this command to the Thessalonian Christians in 1 Thessalonians 5:16. After his command to "rejoice always," Paul then says, "pray without ceasing." You cannot have a relationship with someone if you never talk to that person. How can you have a relationship with God if you never talk to him?

Prayer is more than just asking God for material things. Of course, praying for these things is not necessarily a bad thing...to a slight degree. We cannot let our desires for physical things dictate our prayer life. Instead, we must pray like Jesus tells us to pray. No, I don't mean that we must pray the exact model prayer of Matthew 6:9–13 (though studying this prayer would be well worth your time). I mean that we must pray like Jesus commands us to pray in the previous verses of this context. Matthew 6:7 says, "And when you pray, do not heap up empty phrases as the Gentiles do, for they think that they will be heard for their many words." We don't have to pray like the Gentiles because God already knows what we need. The Gentile's we known for praying unbearably long prayers. A pagan worshipper would speak no less than fifteen minutes of praise to the god or goddess before making his own short and simple request. We do not have to tell God who he is. Believe me, God knows exactly who he is. Praying without ceasing then means praying humbly, having constant conversation with God, and trusting that God will take care of you in every way.

4.   Give thanks. One of the worst qualities a person can possess is being ungrateful. You've met that person before. You know, the one who has literally everything. The one who is so arrogant and rude. Yeah, that person. Ungratefulness is just plain ugly. Paul tells the Thessalonians to "give thanks in all circumstances" (1 Thess 5:18). I bet you can probably think of some circumstances in life where it

would be really difficult to give thanks to God. Let me give you a prime example from my own life.

Before I married my lovely wife, Kayla, I was in two very committed relationships. Of course, these were not going on at the same time. I had other relationships between the end of these two and meeting my wife, but they were here and there and ultimately nowhere. I honestly thought that both of these relationships were going to result in a marriage. But, as you can tell by my being married to someone else, these relationships obviously did not work out. I can tell you with all confidence that the end of these two relationships were incredibly emotionally difficult. I sunk into a deep depression. I wouldn't talk to my family or any of my friends. I stayed locked in my bedroom waiting for life to pass me by. All the while, I knew that the end of these relationships was actually an answer to prayer. The first relationship was with a girl who was not a Christian. The second was with a girl who, thankfully, was a Christian, but our personalities did not match at all. When these relationships ended, the last thing I wanted to do was "give thanks." I wanted to sulk and blame God for not letting them work. But instead, though I was in a deep depression, I tried so very hard to say, "Not my will but yours be done." Ultimately, God led me to my beautiful, smart, talented, amazing wife. Looking back, I can thank God for each event, both good and bad, that has happened in my life. He has worked it together for good. Giving thanks to God in every circumstance is not easy, but it is necessary if we seek to grow in Christ.

5. Grow in knowledge. Remember how I said that part of this progression process was studying your Bible? That's still true, but it's not the end of the story. Study is only beneficial if information is retained. Take studying for a test for example. You brood over your notes and textbook for hours on end until you are finally able to recall the knowledge later. But the marker of great study is not just being

able to recall information for a test. The marker of great study is being able to turn that knowledge into every day wisdom.

The command to "grow in knowledge" is mentioned at least twice in the New Testament: once in Colossians 1:10 and once in 2 Peter 3:18. Both places encourage us to increase in our knowledge of God. The point of these verses, however, does not revolve around the "knowledge" one might gain. Some of us will receive Ph. D.'s in biblical studies while others of us will only read a chapter of the Bible a day. That's fine. Knowledge comes in a variety of different forms. The emphasis then is on *growing* or *increasing* in knowledge. This means putting in the work. This requires time, attention, and patience. Growing is a process. Finding perfection is a process.

Personal Reflection

1) How do you know you are not perfect?
2) John writes that we have an advocate with the Father, Jesus Christ the righteous. What does it mean when we call Jesus our advocate?
3) What are some things you can do to grow closer to God this week?
4) When was the last time you really studied your Bible? Why is it so easy to only read your Bible at church?
5) What are some tools you could use to aid your Bible study?

Appendix: Tools of the Trade

I had originally planned for this book to only be a five-chapter book. About half way through the writing of the previous chapter, I thought it would be beneficial to include an appendix containing the most commonly asked questions I get from new Christians. As I began to whittle down the list of potential questions, I quickly came to realize these questions all deserve their own book. However, I think it necessary to briefly discuss them here. Thus, this section was born. Throughout this section, I will attempt to answer in part the four most commonly asked questions I receive in my ministry from new converts. As has been the custom with this whole book, I have no intention of answering everything in its fullness. I only hope to give you enough sound information so you can study and question even further. Here we go!

What Bible Translation Should I Use?

It is easy to become defensive of "our translation." We tend to believe that our version of the Bible fell from Heaven in a golden parachute and landed directly in our lap. However, it is necessary to take a few steps back and ask some questions concerning our particular translation. Not every translation is created equally. There some versions of the Bible I would certainly recommend you not use. On the other hand, there are others that, if you have these versions, go ahead and use them. Yet, there are still others that I consider my personal favorites. Below is a helpful chart that evaluates translations as they relate to their intended purpose.

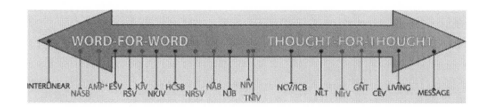

As you search for a Bible translation, ask first, "Do I need something that is more *formally* equivalent or something that is more *functionally* equivalent?" Basically, ask yourself if you need a translation that is true to the original Greek and Hebrew text as closely as possible (formally equivalent) or one that explains the thought of the overall passage (functionally equivalent).

No translation is 100% accurate. This is because there are certain words in every language that cannot be fully translated into another language. Take the word *love* for example. Greek has three words that mean *love*. Each Greek word differs slightly in its meaning. Yet, English has only one word for *love*. This can at times cause an issue in translation. So, the job of the translator is to find the English word or phrase that best fits the intended meaning of the Greek or Hebrew word.

Next, you need to read, or at least reference, the preface to your Bible translation. This will tell you the goal of the translation committee, the intended purpose of your version, and (most of the time) who the translation committee is. In that, the editors of the translation will make clear whether the version is a word-for-word version or a thought-for-thought version. Each version type has its benefits. I use the Message Bible quite frequently as a resource for sermon preparation. However, I will never preach from the Message Bible because it is a paraphrase of the text, not a translation. It is a thought-for-thought version, not a word-for-word translation. I use it as a reference because I like to look at how a group of people understood the overall theme of the text. Sometimes I agree with them. Many times, I disagree with the editors of the Message. All in all, consulting other sources and other versions than your personal favorite will help you grow as a Christian.

You may be looking at your own Bible wondering, "Is this a good Bible? What if I have the wrong one?" Well, the best Bible is a read Bible, so be sure to read your Bible! Here are my big 4 versions (these are the four English versions I use the most often): New American Standard Bible, Christian Standard Bible, English Standard Version, and New King James Version.

You may have noticed that the New International Version (a version many of you likely have) was not on my list. If you use the NIV, that is perfectly okay. The reason I do not use it is because the goal of the NIV committee is an impossible task. The NIV committee sought to form a translation that could be used by all English speakers throughout the world. However, English in America is much different than the English in Europe, Australia, or New Zealand. Take the word *napkin* for example. A *napkin* in America is a piece of cloth or piece of paper used to wipe the mouth after a meal (this is called a *serviette* elsewhere). However, in Australia and New Zealand, a *napkin* is what babies wear to stop a mess when they use the bathroom (this is called a *diaper* in America). See the issue? So, for that reason (i.e., the fluidity of words based on locational context), I do not like using the NIV. Again, that's just my personal preference.

I would recommend you use a word-for-word translation. Consult the chart above for a list of these versions. Word-for-word translations (formally equivalent) will stay true to the original text and will allow you to have a deeper grasp of word study and syntax (i.e., how words function in a sentence). Thought-for-thought translations should only be used for personal devotion and as a secondary resource.

Which Congregation Should I Attend?

Now that you are in Christ, it is vitally important that you worship God on a regular basis with your Christian brothers and sisters. Refusing to do this is warned against in Hebrews 10:25 where the author says we should not "forsake the assembling of ourselves together." Unfortunately, a congregation of the Lord's church may not be a sound or scriptural congregation. How will we know where we should worship?

Understand, not every building that says "Church of Christ" on its sign is a scripturally sound congregation. Before we address what a sound congregation looks like, let's first establish what the church of Jesus Christ actually is.

First, the *church of Christ* is not a title. Though we see it on signs and church buildings, the designation of *church of Christ* is a descriptive term. It is a term of possession. In other words, we (the church) belong to Christ. We are Christ's church. We are his body. Second, the *church of Christ* is not a denomination. There is much discussion today about this issue. However, there is only one church found in Scripture—the true body of Christ. The body of Christ is never to be divided. The word *denominate* (from which we get the word *denomination*) literally means to divide. Therefore, if you are worshipping in a congregation that considers itself a denomination, you are worshipping in a place that acknowledges themselves as ones who have formed a division in the body of Christ. That can't be right.

The body of Christ has several different names found in Scripture. These names are listed below.

1. The church (Acts 8:1)
2. The Kingdom of God (Mark 1:15)
3. The Kingdom of Heaven (Matt 13:24ff)
4. The church of God (1 Cor 1:2)
5. The body of Christ (Eph 1:22)
6. The churches of Christ (Rom 16:16)

7. And "my church" spoken by Jesus (Matt 16:18)

The Bible tells us that the church is the **body** of Christ and the **bride** of Christ. When Jesus returns, he is coming back for his bride and his body. It is vital that the congregation with which we worship is a part of the body of Christ.

So, what makes a *sound* congregation? This question cannot be fully addressed here. However, I do want to give you some criteria that you can use if you are looking for a *sound* congregation.

The congregation must do everything in accordance with the scriptures. This includes the congregation's leadership (having elders and deacons), worship (taking the Lord's Supper every Sunday according to Acts 20:7, worshiping without instruments according to Eph 5:19), and teaching. If the congregation promotes the teaching of any false doctrine, you need to leave. If the congregation worships in a way that is not in harmony with Scripture, then you need to seek out another congregation. If the congregation does not teach baptism as a necessity to receive full salvation, you need to find another congregation. There are certainly other issues that could be discussed here as well, but space does not permit such an endeavor. All this means that you need to know your Bible and what it actually says. The church is not marked by the words that are found on the sign outside the building. The church is the people who are clothed in Christ.

How Can I Be Taken Seriously in My Congregation?

I think there are three Scriptures that will answer this question for us. The first is 1 Tim 4:12. "Let no one despise your youth, but be an example in speech, in conduct, in love, in faith, and in purity." We know that no one should "despise our youth" or look down on us because of our age, but *why* should no one despise our youth? Paul says that young people are to be an example in five categories: in speech (how you talk), in conduct (how you act), in love (how you bond), in faith (how you practice what you preach), and in purity (how you treat yourself and others). So, step one is to be an example to all those around you—both young and old.

1 Peter 5:5 follows a discourse of what Peter has said to the elders who are leading at this time. Peter then turns his attention to those who are younger saying, "Likewise, you who are younger, be subject to the elders. Clothe yourselves, all of you, with humility toward one another, for 'God opposes the proud but gives grace to the humble.'" Part of being an example is being humble. It is easy to become puffed up and proud when we are young. We think we know everything about anything. Therefore, it is vitally necessary that we humble ourselves to the leadership of the church and to the headship of Christ. This means both being a person of submission and support.

Lastly, Hebrews 10:24–25 admonishes us to make assembling with the saints a priority. We are to do this so we can "stir up one another in love and in good works." If you want to be taken seriously in the church then you need to show up to church! You will not be taken seriously if you are not present with the saints. Be involved! Show up because you love the Lord. How can you be taken more seriously as a new Christian in your congregation? Show up, be humble, and be an example.

Why Do I/Should I Compare Myself to Others

Individuality might be the most glorified virtue in today's modern world. You should feel free to be your own individual person. God created you with your own wonderful personality. That being said, comparison is not always a bad thing—though most of the time we view it as something bad. We compare ourselves to the girl who is skinnier than us or to the guy with bigger muscles than we have. In my case, I compare myself to the author who has sold more copies of his book. But comparison, when used appropriately, is not always bad.

In 1 Corinthians 11:1, Paul writes, "Be imitators of me as I am of Christ." That is a comparison! The Corinthians had not actually seen or met Christ (at least we aren't led to believe they had). They did not have Jesus as a tangible example. Thus, Paul tells them to do just as he does. Paul is saying, "Compare yourself to me because I am comparing myself to the Lord."

We need to ask ourselves the same question Paul asks in Galatians 1:10. "For am I now seeking the approval of man or of God? Or am I trying to please man? If I were still trying to please man, I would not be a servant of Christ." Who is the source of our approval? Who is the standard for our comparison? Am I comparing myself to the standard of God or the standard of people?

All that being said, if one is asking the question above concerning the comparison of oneself to others because of physical things (e.g., you think someone is prettier than you or smarter than you), I want to remind you to read Psalm 139:13–15.

> For you formed my inward parts;
> you knitted me together in my mother's womb.
> I praise you, for I am fearfully and wonderfully made.
> Wonderful are your works;
> my soul knows it very well.
> My frame was not hidden from you,
> when I was being made in secret,
> intricately woven in the depths of the earth.

You are wonderfully made! God took his time with you! God loves you! You are special to him!

Personal Reflection

1) How can you be an example to people at church this week?
2) Is your congregation a sound congregation? What can you do to teach truth if it is not?
3) What do you like about your Bible translation? Will you get a new one? Why or why not?
4) Could someone who doesn't know Jesus look at your life and know what it means to be a Christian?
5) How do you know that you are fearfully and wonderfully made?